Living Faith

"As I read the books of Helen Roseveare, these powerful words come to my mind – REALITY, VISION, INTEGRITY, COURAGE, ACTION and FORGIVENESS. They are all words that we need to hold centrally in our lives too. Perhaps you don't read many books but I would urge you to read this one - and then to share what you've learned with others. They are a huge challenge to the indifference and lukewarm-ness of our day. It is necessary for the church to have IMPACT for the good of this world. Helen shows what kind of impact you too can have."

George Verwer

Living Faith

*Willing to be stirred
as a pot of paint*

Helen Roseveare

CHRISTIAN
FOCUS

Contents

Dedication 7
Preface 9

Prologue *(Hebrews 11:1, 6)* 11

   1. Stir Me to Give *(Hebrews 11:4-7)* 41

   2. Stir Me to Go *(Hebrews 11:8-19)* 87

   3. Stir Me To Pray *(Hebrews 11:24-31)* 147

Epilogue *(Hebrews 11:32-40)* 197
About the Author 213

To
the team at Nebobongo,
nationals and foreigners,
where many of these truths were learned.

PREFACE

Many friends, both at home and overseas, have suggested that I write the substance of the many talks given during my deputation ministry. I am indeed grateful to each one who has urged me to complete the task.

After much prayer and discussion, I have considered it wise to change the names of certain Africans to hide their identities from their national colleagues; where there is any reason to fear they could be harmed. If some readers recognize certain people by their testimonies, heard elsewhere, and are thereby puzzled by an unknown name, please accept this explanation. The testimonies remain true but the identities are not revealed.

Conversations, especially with Africans, have been reconstructed as translated from the local languages, to give the true gist of what was said, but I do not pretend that these are verbatim quotations. They are as nearly accurate as I can remember them in order to make real-life situations live.

In verse three of the hymn that gives the basic structure to the book, "Stir me, oh! stir me, Lord," one word in line two has been changed from the original "till prayer is joy, till prayer turns into praise" to read "till prayer is power, till prayer turns into praise."

Helen Roseveare

LIVING FAITH

Stir me, oh! stir me, Lord, I care not how,
But stir my heart in passion for the world:
Stir me to *give*, to *go*, but most to *pray*:
Stir till the blood-red banner be unfurled
O'er lands that still in heathen darkness lie,
O'er deserts where no cross is lifted high.

Stir me, oh! stir me, Lord, till all my heart
Is filled with strong compassion for these souls;
Till Thy compelling Word drives me to pray;
Till Thy constraining love reach to the poles
Far north and south, in burning deep desire,
Till east and west are caught in love's great fire.

Stir me, oh! stir me, Lord, till prayer is pain,
Till prayer is power, till prayer turns into praise:
Stir me till heart and will and mind, yea all
Is wholly Thine to use through all the days.
Stir, till I learn to pray exceedingly:
Stir till I learn to wait expectantly.

Stir me, oh! stir me, Lord, Thy heart was stirred
By love's intensest fire, till Thou didst give
Thine only Son, Thy best beloved One,
E'en to the dreadful cross, that I might live.
Stir me to give myself so back to Thee,
That Thou canst give Thyself again through me.

Stir me, oh! stir me, Lord, for I can see
Thy glorious triumph; day begin to break;
The dawn already gilds the eastern sky:
Oh, Church of Christ, arise, awake, awake;
Oh! stir us, Lord, as heralds of that day,
For night is past, our King is on His way.

Mrs. A Head

*As God says to us through Peter, "I think it meet (right),
as long as I am in this tabernacle [with you] to stir you up"*
(2 Pet. 1:13 KJV).

PROLOGUE

FAITH – GOD'S GIFT TO US

Now faith is being sure of what we hope for and certain of what we do not see. This is what the ancients were commended for...

.. without faith it is impossible to please God, because anyone who comes to him must believe that he exists and that he rewards those who earnestly seek him (Heb. 11:1-2, 6 NIV).

For it is by grace you have been saved, through faith and this not from yourselves, it is the gift of God-not by works, so that no one can boast (Eph. 2:8-9 NIV).

"I dare you!"

With a tight knot in my stomach, teeth clenched, and eyes screwed shut, I jumped – and waited – and it was all right!

I opened my eyes, looked disdainfully at my brother and sister, and turned abruptly to walk away so they would not see me being sick.

Why did they do it? Why did they pick on me, daring me to do this or that, just because they knew I was scared? But I would not let them know! No, somehow I would conquer that awful inner shrinking, that panic that threatened to overwhelm me every time that they egged me on. That time it had only been to jump off a six-foot wall. The silly thing was that I had done it before without any nervousness; but when they said, "Dare you" the realization that perhaps there was a danger hit me so forcibly that I could hardly think straight.

This vivid imagination, picturing all sorts of horrors as the result of minor incidents, never left me. I grew up with "fear" just around the corner. I could even manage to be afraid of happiness, in case it went away and became illusory.

"Dare you!"

The taunt in his voice cut me, the insolence in his eyes frightened me. The group stood over me, menacingly, in the dirty hallway. There were footsteps outside, and everyone froze. Time hung in the still air. The footsteps passed – and faded – and they let out their breath.

"Do you promise not to squeal on us?"

He did not actually threaten me; he did not need to strike me again. I crouched back into the dark corner, wrapped in the shame of my cowardice.

'Yes," I whispered miserably.

"Come on," snarled the leader, kicking my already sore shins. "She isn't worth beating up! Let's get out of here!"

The gang left. I lay, miserable and lonely, until I had to be sick. I staggered up the rickety stairs to the bathroom. It was eleven o'clock at night.

Why, why had I got involved with this East London gang? I had not wanted or expected this, when I had offered to help the Anglican Franciscan fathers in their relief work in Peckham. I had wanted to "do something for the war effort" during my school summer holiday. For a week I had served soup in a large air raid shelter. I had visited homes along three or four roads, filling in questionnaires about each householder's need for help, food, coal, or sickness benefits. I had been with Father Charles Preston to visit a boys' reformatory.

Then one evening each week, I was asked to remain in the small home of the Fathers, while they were at prayers in the beautiful chapel across the road, to "host" a club of senior teenagers. These young folk had mostly been turned away from the local community club because of their police records. All I had to do, so I was told, was to change the records on the phonograph and replenish the cart of drinks from the kitchen. That had been all that I had to do the first week, but this week, things had subtly turned nasty.

I went into the front room where the club had met earlier that evening. The smell of alcohol and cigarette smoke filled the fetid air. The turntable was still revolving, the needle scratching endlessly around the centre of the record. Instinctively I moved to turn it off, subconsciously irritated by the sound. I kept my eyes from the far corner, while automatically gathering up glasses and bottles. That was where they had attacked the girl, fallen on her, dragging her clothes off her ... Why hadn't I rushed for authority? Why hadn't I screamed for help? I felt sick again. The big one had had a knife.

I suppose I had moved. He had swung around and seen me. With venomous anger, he had flung the knife. I had ducked and dived for the door, but he caught me, twisting my arm behind me viciously.

I do not know what would have happened next, had he not heard that whistle. The whole gang had frozen in total silence. Then suddenly everything seemed to happen at once. The light was switched off. I was flung down the stairs. The gang was there as soon as I was and pinned me down.

You speak a word of this, and we'll ..."

He had boxed my ears, sending me to the ground as I struggled to stand. My head was splitting. I was drunk with fear. Unbelievable, horrified fear.

I glanced to that corner behind the sofa now. She was not there. I do not know how or when she left. I was alone. I shivered and rushed to the bathroom to be sick again.

☼✦☼✦☼✦☼

I started my studies as a first-year medical student. I will never forget that first day in the anatomy dissection room. I was really very ignorant as to what university life was all about. I just knew that I wanted to do well. I meant to work hard. I hoped desperately that the nagging fear in the background would stay in the background. I did not understand it, nor did I want to look at it and analyze it. I just wished it were not there. Perhaps it was compounded of loneliness, a sense of inadequacy, and the dread of failure.

Watching hundreds of unknown others, I did as they did, padlocking my bicycle to a slot in the railings. I pulled my satchel from the basket, with the as yet unstained first volume of Cunningham's *Anatomical Dissection* and the small canvas bag of dissection instruments. Merging with the stream entering the anatomy department building, I took a white coat from a peg in the corridor, exchanging it for my jacket. A strange *something* was in the air. The hairs on the back of my neck began to prickle. The old nausea of fear was welling up. I willed it down. We passed through the swinging doors into another corridor, turned right through another door – and I was wrapped in 'it.' It? Even now, as I think of that moment, I can smell it and sense it and feel it. Numb horror tightened the knot in my stomach. If there had not been more and more students pouring through the door, carrying me relentlessly forward to the far end of the hall, between the rows of tables with their silent, grey, formalin-soaked "occupants," I would have turned and fled.

It was the smell – that formalin-heavy odour – that pricked eyes and nose and throat. That smell haunted me, stuck to me, followed me. That smell spoke to me of those bodies. That smell laughed at my stumbling fingers. That smell stirred up all my fears. All the effort of learning, of trying to understand and appreciate the mysteries of the human body, was plagued by that smell. When the assistants came to examine us at each stage of the dissection, that smell drove what little I had learned from my memory. It mocked me into silence. I could not answer even the simplest question.

I knew I was in the wrong place. That smell confirmed it. I would never be a doctor. That smell assured me of the fact. And yet it was that smell that kept me there till I succeeded. Strange! It was almost as though the heavy sickly smell had said to me: "I dare you ..." – to leave medicine? to change courses? to acknowledge defeat? Despite everything. I stuck to it!

✿✦✿✦✿✦✿

"Dare you trust Me?"

It was just one way in which the Holy Spirit began to work in my heart to convince me of my need of the Saviour.

Years before, I had begun to feel the need of acknowledging God. I needed a God who could give meaning to life and direction and control to living. At that time I had latched onto a particular group who believed in strict discipline and clearly defined rules; I had found security in this. They made the decisions. I just had to obey. The responsibility was theirs, and they promised a lifelong sense of belonging.

Then there had come the phase of questioning the very existence of God. Was He only a psychological crutch, "the opiate of the people," as some said? Did I only believe in Him because I dared not be honest enough to disbelieve, as others suggested? Many in our classes mocked those of us who still believed in God, calling us old-fashioned, unscientific, the mental prisoners of a Victorian upbringing.

"Dare you step out and be honest? There is no God. You deceive yourself, because you haven't the courage to face the truth."

"Dare you ...?"

I had hesitatingly, half-heartedly, tried. I joined discussion groups who aired their views on scientific philosophies and left God out. In secret I still went to church early every Sunday, afraid to leave Him out altogether in case we were wrong... and anyway, without God, life was suddenly desperately insecure. There were no absolute values left; there was no direction or reason for living. Scientific or atheistic "post-Christian" humanists told me that I dared not believe in God merely because I was "poorly integrated" or "insecure" or simply "ignorant."

"Dare you ...?"

"Dare you not ...?"

✧✦✧✦✧✦✧

The quiet, consistent, happy lives of Christian students drew me and began to convince me. The teaching in their Bible study groups and the assurance in their daily prayer meetings brought a sense of sober reality. They talked of faith as an objective reality, not a blind leap-in-the-dark, hoping for the best. Faith to them was something far more wonderful and real than mere believism or frightened escapism. They spoke of faith as a fact, a gift from God Himself to His people to enable them to grasp and comprehend truth.

"This faith," they said, "is something far more durable and wonderful than the inborn instinctive 'faith' that accompanies all living, such as that which enables you to sit on a chair, trusting the workmanship of the carpenter and the strength of the structure to support you, without undue questioning."

I began to listen and to question, to ponder and to meditate around this word *faith*, the faith of God. Using a small concordance, I started to look up all the references to it in the Bible, seeking for an understanding at first, then searching for a means to obtain this same gift of God.

I found people in the Old Testament who were enabled to believe in God with an unshakeable steadfastness; the Israelites leaned on Him and had confidence in Him. This aspect of trust obviously came out of an absolute assurance that the One they trusted was trustworthy, and would not let them down or fail them or change His word. Oh, yes, I could understand believing in a God like that.

I found another line of thought running all through the Bible, linked with faith. Starting with Abraham, I found that he believed in God and His promises, and because of that belief, God accepted him and called him righteous. The harlot Rahab believed in the same God, and her trust saved her from destruction. David, having committed adultery and manslaughter, reached through to an assurance of forgiveness of sin by committing himself wholly to the judgment of the righteous God. The prophet Habakkuk summed it all up:

The just shall live by his faith (Hab. 2:4).

People who obtain righteousness in exchange for their sinfulness by believing in God shall live, fully live, as God meant them to live. They shall have life – abundant, spiritual life – as they live in that faith that alone can make them righteous.

I moved into the New Testament and read through Paul's letters to the Romans and to the Galatians. Then I turned to the letters to Timothy and to the Hebrews and to the letter of James. I went back again to the gospel according to John until I came to a verse near the end which said:

These things are written, that ye might believe that Jesus is the Christ, the Son of God; and that believing ye might have life through his name (John 20:31).

I remembered reading in the letter to the Romans:

So then faith cometh by hearing, and hearing by the word of God (Rom. 10:17).

I re-read John's gospel, during the December of 1944. Right from the start, the writer talks of our need to believe and stresses that we *can* believe. John the Baptist told us of the Light, the true light that shines in our darkness "that all men through him might believe." He declared that "as many as received him, to them gave he power to become the sons of God, even to them that believe on his name."

A hunger was stirring. To be loved by God as His child sounded wonderful. Could it he true? As I read of various miracles, I saw that it was when Jesus changed the water to wine at the wedding of Cana in Galilee that His disciples put their faith in Him. When He healed the sick son of the royal official at Capernaum, by a spoken word of authority, the official and all his household believed.

When Jesus fed five thousand people with a boy's picnic lunch of five small loaves and two small fish, the people marvelled. When He raised Lazarus from the dead, calling him out of the tomb on the fourth day after his burial, all wrapped about with the burial clothes, many of the Jews put their faith in Jesus.

Suddenly I came on some startling verses in chapter six:

I am the bread of life: he that cometh to me shall never hunger; and he that believeth on me shall never thirst (John 6:35).

And this is the will of him that sent me, that every one which seeth the Son, and believeth on him, may have everlasting life: and I will raise him up at the last day (John 6:40).

The passage went on to say:

Except ye eat the flesh of the Son of man, and drink his blood, ye have no life in you (John 6:53).

Already there was a stirring in my heart, a reaching out to grasp the inner meaning of the words, to satisfy a deep-seated hunger.

When Jesus was teaching at the great feast, He reminded those present of the many miracles He had already performed in their midst. If they could not believe in His words, could they not believe the evidence of their eyes in His works?

"And many believed on him," we read (John 10:42).

As I read on, I could hardly believe that the Pharisees sent soldiers to take Jesus into custody!

The tremendous story of the healing of the man born blind excited me, especially his own words of testimony: *"Whether he be a sinner or no, I know not: one thing I know, that, whereas I was blind, now I see."* The crass stupidity of the Pharisees, their insults and petty self-righteousness, annoyed me. Already I longed that my inner eyes, the eyes of my heart, might be opened to see the Lord, as that man did. I longed to believe. I prayed to believe. I read more and more every day in order to believe. I talked with others and asked endless questions that I might believe.

Many of the Jews … believed on Jesus (John 12:11).

What stopped me? What held me back from doing just that? It was what I wanted to do.

Jesus continued to warn His disciples that in the coming days He must die, saying:

Except a corn of wheat fall into the ground and die, it abideth alone: but if it die, it bringeth forth much fruit (John 12:24).

And as a result of His continued teaching "among the chief rulers also many believed on him."

As I read on through the story of the supper in the upper room and of Judas' betrayal, I came to the tragedy of Peter's denial when he swore that he did not know Jesus. Only a few chapters before, he had publicly declared that he would lay down his life for his Lord!

A flicker of fear caught my heart. Was this what held me back? Would I not have done just as Peter did? I would fail Him too. I was beginning to believe in Him, but could I ever be faithful? Would my faith in the Lord stand up to tests like that?

I read on through the heartbreaking account of the trial and the flogging, the mockery, and the sentence. I judged Pilate's weakness with scorn and all the injustice that he allowed yet I dreaded to think what I would have done in that setting and those circumstances.

Through all the record of the crucifixion, the silent dignity of the unresisting, holy, innocent Man stood out in stark contrast to all the evil and cunning, the envy and hatred around Him. The sheer, barbaric cruelty, the thought of the agony of physical pain, the realization of total, human injustice, these only highlighted the quiet triumph as Jesus cried out, *"It is finished!"*

What was finished? Whatever it was, it enabled Christ then to give up His life. He died, and He was taken down from the cross and buried.

The twentieth chapter of John's gospel gripped me as though I had never heard the story before. Christ rose again. He appeared to Mary and then to His disciples. He was alive! Thomas could not believe it – no, I guess I would not have believed it either. Thomas had to see and to touch in order to believe.

Then Jesus said to him, *"Because thou hast seen me, thou hast believed: blessed are they that have not seen, and yet have believed."*

Oh, how much I wanted to believe!

At the end of the book, I came again to that verse that I had read weeks earlier:

These are written, that ye might believe that Jesus is the Christ, the Son of God; and that believing ye might have life through his name (John 20:31).

It was becoming very clear. My head and mind and understanding agreed, but somehow I did not "know for sure without a shadow of doubt" (which someone told me was the real meaning of to believe). I did not *know* Jesus. I found that I did believe that He was the Christ, the Son of God, but something was missing. My faith, if it were yet faith, was not living, vital, real. It was only theoretical.

I remember that during that term at college, some of the members of the Christian Union had been studying the eleventh chapter of the letter to the Hebrews, preparing for the following term's meetings. Perhaps sensing something of the hunger in my heart, they had invited me to join them. I do not remember anything of the first study, despite my urgent interest in the subject of faith.

Now faith is the substance of things hoped for, the evidence of things not seen (Heb. 11:1).

But I do remember how startled I was at some of what was said and discussed at the second study on verse three: *"Through faith we understand that the worlds were framed by the word of God, so that things which are seen were not made of things which do appear."*

They said that God had spoken a word of command: "Let there be light," and there was light. This made sense ... as did so much else.

When I left the Bible study group that evening and went back to my own room, I began to question it all. How could I believe such – what was I about to say – rubbish? Yet ten minutes earlier my mind had accepted that it was sense. What made me change so easily? Using five normal senses in a logical scientific manner, I was prepared to say now that it was nonsensical. Yet such a short time previously, in the atmosphere of a Christian Bible study group, was it some sixth sense that had assured me that it was true, that God had created the world that we see from nothing? The student leader had explained that nothing was not something called nothing; it was actually nothing, the absence of something. God had created this perfect, orderly, beautiful world by a word of command: "Let there be ..." and there was.

Through the term, we had moved on through chapter eleven of the letter to the Hebrews, looking at different illustrations of the outworking of the principles of faith.

By faith Abel, Enoch and Noah worshipped and served God. By faith Abraham, Isaac, Jacob and Joseph praised and obeyed God. By faith Moses chose to go God's way instead of the world's. By faith the walls of Jericho fell. Throughout, we saw faith as a driving force, an activity born out of an assurance of God, out of a conviction in the fact of God and the activities of God.

Some of the girls had devotional books to help them in these studies, and I borrowed some. In a book by G. Campbell Morgan I read: "Life has dimensions other than those that can be encompassed by the senses, and into those dimensions nothing can enter except the principle of faith." In the great realm of *life* – abundant, full living – there is obviously so much beyond the five senses and the measurements and definitions of science. Here faith is the active force, the sixth sense.

Going back to the first verse of the eleventh chapter of the letter to the Hebrews, where we find the only definition of faith that the Bible gives, we read: *"Faith is the substance of things hoped for, the evidence of things not seen."* A conviction is worked in our hearts and consciousness that God is, and that God is active in all the realm of living beyond the five senses. This conviction gives to us an assurance concerning the things hoped for, as yet unseen and indefinable perhaps, yet vitally real and certain to the realm of faith.

During my Christmas vacation in 1944–45, I went to a Christian house party in London. A certain Miss Doris Candy, well remembered and loved by many of us to this day, led us in a Bible study in the book of Genesis at the beginning of the week. I was fascinated, but also appalled at my ignorance. How did she know her Bible so well? She made the story live, with great relevance to us right then. I felt I knew nothing, as she unfolded to us riches from the Word of God. Later in the week she was to do a similar study in Paul's letter to the Romans, and she suggested that we read it by ourselves first, so as to derive more benefit from her teaching. I determined to do so. I sat up all one night, reading and answering questions on each part, as directed in a study book someone gave me (*Search the Scriptures*, IVP).

In the very first chapter I came up against this important word again – *faith*. "The gospel ... is the power of God unto salvation to every one that believeth," that is, to every one who has faith. Chapter after chapter unfolded this gospel – the righteousness of God imputed to me *if* I believed. I found no difficulty in following the argument that all men were sinners in the sight of God. To me it was obvious that we all fell short of His holy standard, His true righteousness.

> *But now the righteousness of God ... which is by faith of Jesus Christ unto all and upon all them that believe: ....being justified freely by his grace, through the redemption that is in Christ Jesus: Whom God hath set forth to be a propitiation through faith in his blood* (Rom. 3:21-25).

As James Philip clearly states: "The Apostle, having concluded the whole world accountable to God, announces the amazing fact that God the Judge acquits the guilty, granting him a free pardon and a new beginning, and making him a new creature in Christ." Something in me reached out and grasped at this extraordinary and wonderful statement of fact. There actually was a redemption, a propitiation. The ransom had been paid "by Christ Jesus ... in His Blood." It was something already completed. This was what I had read in John's gospel. Jesus Christ had paid our ransom on the cross when He was crucified, when He poured out His life's blood until He died. "The redemption that came ..."– aorist tense, a finished, past act. Suddenly I understood that cry of Christ's on the cross: *"It is finished!"* It was redemption that was finished. The ransom price for sinners had been paid fully. The death sentence on sin was passed and carried out. "Justified" could be written against my name, as the sin bearer gave up His life for me. He paid the whole price. Nothing was lacking.

I read on excitedly, all through that night until the early hours of the morning. My heart was strongly moved, as though on fire. I had glimpsed a great light, and yet somehow I felt blinded by it. Something was escaping my grasp. An almost desperate desire was forcing me to extend my reach. The following day, Miss Candy took us through the letter to the Romans systematically, but strangely I did not want the correctness just then. The fire had touched me, and I was terrified that the spark might go out before it had time to blaze up and set me truly alight.

I went to see her later that day. I plunged straight in with one hungry question.

"How do I get faith? How do I know that I have faith? What is faith, anyway?"

Quietly she sorted me out, seeking to discover how much I did or did not know already. Together we went through the gospel story.

"Do you believe that Jesus was the Son of God?"

"Yes," I answered with a sudden, certain conviction.

"Do you believe that He died on the cross of Calvary?"

"Yes." I had no doubt of that.

"Do you believe that He rose again from the dead?"

"Yes" – the evidence seemed incontrovertible.

"Do you believe that Jesus died as a ransom for the sins of men?"

Miss Candy explained the phrase. She read certain other verses to me, as from Paul's letter to the Romans:

For all have sinned, and come short of the glory of God
(3:23)

and,

The wages of sin is death; but the gift of God is eternal life
through Jesus Christ our Lord (6:23).

Oh, yes, I had read these verses last night and clearly accepted them.

For God so loved the world, that he gave his only begotten
Son, that whosoever believeth in him should not perish, but
have everlasting life (John 3:16).

For even the Son of man came not to be ministered unto,
but to minister, and to give his life a ransom for many
(Mark 10:45).

There were other verses, but these are the ones that stayed in my mind and linked together to speak peace to my heart.

Yes, I did believe all that, and yet somehow I lacked *faith* that it was really for *me*, and not just for everyone else. I so urgently needed assurance in my own heart.

"But you believe in God?" Miss Candy remonstrated patiently.

Yes, of course I did. I doubt if I had ever actually disbelieved, even when I was trying to "do without Him" those last six months.

"Could God lie?"

No, that was certain. God, if He were God, obviously would not lie. He simply would not be God if He did.

"Well, He has said, *'Whosoever believeth in him.'* You believe in Him and in His death as a ransom for sin. Are you not part of that 'whosoever'?"

Yes, I could see the logic. I knew that I did believe. What was worrying me? Why did I doubt that I had faith?

"Faith is God's gift in your heart that has made you able to believe," she explained, and then read to me from another of Paul's letters: *"For by grace are ye saved through faith; and that not of yourselves: it is the gift of God: not of works, Lest any man should boast"* – unmerited mercy and love reaching out to save me from my sins, and planting in my heart His faith that I might be able to believe it!

Could this possibly be?

The supper bell rang, and we went down to the hurly-burly noise of a big crowd of girls, chatting and laughing. During supper, an argument developed over the understanding of the phrase "This is my body" said by the Lord Jesus of Himself as the Bread of Life. Already on edge, fighting my own internal battle toward faith, I was irritated by the discussion. I got heated and spoke angrily. Some looked at me, amused, others, surprised. One or two were frankly distressed at my outburst. Feeling ashamed, I left the table hurriedly and went upstairs on my own.

I flung myself on my bed and cried out to God in my heartache. I wanted Him so badly to be my friend and my Saviour. I longed for His gift of faith that I might not only believe but know that I had received forgiveness.

Be still, and know that I am God (Ps. 46:10).

I had glanced up through my tears at the painted text on the wall over my bed, and God spoke to me.

"Stop struggling, and searching, and asking. Just KNOW ..."

And I knew. In that moment He filled me with His gift of faith. I knew Him. I knew His love, His nearness, His forgiveness. A great happiness filled me, and peace seemed to take over all my senses. I cried with relief; the struggle was over. I believed; I believed into the faith; I believed into the redemption wrought for me by the death of Jesus Christ, God's only Son, on the cross at Calvary. I knew that I was forgiven, accepted, loved by God. I knew nothing of the doctrine of adoption then, but I sensed that He owned me, as a father his child.

I went downstairs to the evening meeting, in a strangely embarrassed state. I knew I was happy, but for once I had no words to express my feelings. It was the last meeting of the house party; tomorrow all would be going home.

After some singing Mrs Gilbart-Smith, the leader, asked for testimonies. I was not sure what that expression meant and waited in silence. Nothing happened. She again invited the girls to take part, to share of their experiences. Again, a slightly strained, uneasy silence.

"Has no one met with God during this week together?" she asked.

"Oh, yes," I blurted out, "I have!"

I got no further. Suddenly I did not know what to say, how to express the extraordinary sense of certainty and peace and joy that seemed to flood me. Tears were welling up in my eyes. If I said another word, they would spill over. I knew God. That was the one overwhelming fact.

"Be still, and know ... God."

I did.

What had I read the day before in Romans?

The word of faith ... that if thou shalt confess with thy mouth the Lord Jesus, and shalt believe in thy heart that God hath raised him from the dead, thou shalt be saved (Rom. 10:8-9).

I was saved and knew I was.

How had faith come? Where had it come from? How did I put this faith into action and believe? I did not then try to puzzle it out.

Faith cometh by hearing, and hearing by the word of God (Rom. 10:17).

Later, I read how Nygren puts it: "When one hears the gospel and is conquered by it, that is faith!" and that just expressed it for me.

✿✦✿✦✿✦✿

The next six months were exciting. I knew from the moment that I was saved that I would have to give to the Lord Jesus Christ one hundred per cent loyal service. I was conquered by the gospel. I loved my new Master with a deep inner passion of loving, and that love had to be expressed in active service. The faith of God in my heart was a burning reality that had to work, to do, to *live*.

I have never seen a contradiction between the clear teaching in the fourth chapter of the letter of Paul to the Romans, that saving faith is independent of works, and the equally clear statements in the second chapter of the letter of James to the twelve tribes, that living faith must he manifested by deeds. This seems obvious. I knew only too well that I was not saved by anything I had done or achieved, not even by my believing, but only by God's gift of His faith in my heart, enabling me to believe that Jesus Christ had done all that had to be done to ransom my guilty soul. In Him I was redeemed and that freely by grace, unmerited mercy. But I knew equally certainly that to express my gratitude, the upwelling love in my heart, to respond to this so-great salvation, I *must* show my newfound faith by living deeds.

July 1946 found me at the Keswick Convention in the Lake District of northwest England in a small camping party of about fifteen girls, among the five thousand Christians who gathered for a week of Bible teaching. On Friday morning, the group of us sat in the central block of the vast marquee, directly facing the platform, perhaps some twelve rows from the front. The singing was tremendous. After five days of endless rain, the sun had broken through, and the glory outside seemed reflected by the joy inside the tent. Several missionaries gave short telling testimonies to God's blessing in different parts of the world, and each one ended by stressing the great need for other young lives to join them, if the gospel were ever to be preached to the uttermost parts of the earth in our generation. The final speaker drew it all together, pleading with us to surrender our all to the Lord Jesus Christ, who had given His all, His life, to redeem us.

He challenged us with the words of Christ:

> *Whosoever he be of you that forsaketh not all that he hath, he cannot be my disciple* (Luke 14:33).

The leader of the meeting continued: "Do you want the inestimable privilege of being His disciple, His co-labourer, thrust out into His harvest field? As we sing the next hymn, if you are willing to say *yes* to Him on His terms and go anywhere He sends you, will you stand?"

The great congregation remained seated with heads bowed to sing a hymn that became from that day the prayer of my heart:

> Stir me, oh! stir me, Lord, I care not how,
> But stir my heart in passion for the world.

Unknown to me, I had been waiting for this moment. Every part of me tingled with fervent joy and happiness that I was allowed the privilege of responding, and that Christ was inviting *me* to serve *Him*, to be called His ambassador, His missionary. With over one hundred others I stood, without the least sense of pressure or of strain. At that moment, there was not even a trace of fear or of hesitation. I just knew that *this* was what I wanted with all my being – a means to put faith into action, living faith, to say thank you in some tiny way for the great gift of His faith, so freely given to me by His grace.

After the service, I slipped away from the group and made my way up the lower slopes of Skiddaw. I sat there alone in the bracken, gazing out over the valley and the lake to the distant mountains; a precious stillness hung in the sun-drenched air. For two or three hours I stayed there, in tune with God and unbelievably happy in the consciousness of direction, in a confirmation of the inner urge to missionary service that had been growing in me during the previous eighteen months.

I again went to Keswick the following year. There had been various battles during the year, even moments of uncertainty as to whether what I understood to be my "missionary call" was perhaps only an emotional response of my own nature and not really a vocational direction from God at all. Would it stand the test of time? Could I go through with what might be involved? Missionary speakers had come to our College Christian Union almost every month, as also to the university missionary breakfasts. I had listened avidly to each one. I had read the biographies and literature that they brought with them, but these tended to frighten rather than to encourage me. As I read of places of loneliness, I was very conscious of my own need of friendships. As I read of the struggles of others over language study and communications, I could not help but remember that I had failed to learn French at school and had only just scraped through Latin. Besides which, one of my chief difficulties was an overriding shyness and consequent inability to communicate in English, let alone in a foreign language. I was not really troubled by the thought of doing without some of the world's luxuries, or even having to "rough it" in a primitive situation. My parents had never indulged us by an extravagant use of money; we had spent most of our annual family holidays under canvas "roughing it" in the Lake District or on the continent, and the frugalities of strict wartime rationing during my teen years had helped to develop a "do-it-yourself" attitude to the solving of problems. What did scare me, however, was the thought of carrying responsibilities and making decisions that I knew to be beyond my abilities. Maybe there would rarely be colleagues to whom I could turn for advice or help.

The apostle James has also written: *"The trying of your faith worketh patience. But let patience have her perfect work, that ye may be perfect and entire wanting nothing."*

I did not know this verse then, nor that James also says that these trials of our faith should be considered "pure joy!" Certainly I found no joy in the battles against the doubts that began to assail me. Would I not be better suited to a job at home?

As the previous year at Keswick, I went up onto the mountain slope behind the field where we were camping to be alone with God. I sat there and reread the hymn that had so stirred me the previous year. I wanted God's assurance that it was He who was calling me into His service and thrusting me out into His mission field, and not just some emotional responsiveness of my own heart. As I struggled with my problem, repeatedly assuring God that I honestly wanted only to do His will, a sense of peace began to replace the sense of conflict.

Delight thyself also in the LORD;
And he shall give thee the desires of thine heart (Ps. 37:4).

Once more, as the year before, I came to a place of solemn committal to Him. I endeavoured honestly and with a deliberate act of will to lay myself as it were, on the altar, giving all to God, as far as I could understand what that meant. I asked Him to accept my act as a "living sacrifice." I asked Him to help me to become willing to renounce all, to be single-eyed for His will and His glory. I wanted to have no other ambition than to serve Him wholeheartedly. I referred back to the hymn and asked Him to stir me through and through, so that I might be wholly His, no part thought of as my own.

As I lay out on the hillside, in an attempt to consecrate myself wholly to Him and to His service, I seemed to get a brief glimpse of the fight that might lie ahead. In complete sincerity I ended my prayer somewhat as follows: "Please go on working in me until I really am transformed into the image of Your Son. Today I mean this, with every ounce of my being, but when You start doing it, and the stirring hurts, and I feel I can't take any more, maybe I'll cry out to You to stop. Please when that happens, don't listen to my cry to stop, but just remember my vow today to be available to You, and just go on working away at me to make me like You want me to be." I meant that prayer. I still mean it. I longed that the faith that He had put in my heart might be a living faith and never a dead faith.

> *I am crucified with Christ: nevertheless I live; yet not I, but*
> *Christ liveth in me: and the life which I now live in the flesh*
> *I live by the faith of the Son of God, who loved me, and gave*
> *himself for me* (Gal. 2:20).

I would not dare claim that verse as mine, but Paul expresses there the deep aspiration of my heart. I long that it should be true.

✧✦✧✦✧✦✧

Many, many years later, I was reminded vividly of that day on the mountains at Keswick. It was in 1969, three years after missionaries had returned to the northeastern province of Zaire (ex-Belgian Congo) following the devastation of the civil uprising of the "Simba guerrillas" of 1964–65. Together with our African church colleagues, we had started on the long slow process of reconstruction. The story is told in some detail elsewhere of how the five evangelical missionary societies working in the area put all their medical resources and personnel together to "develop a 250-bed hospital with facilities for one thousand outpatients daily, and first-class medical and surgical, obstetric and paediatric care ... (supporting) a training school for twenty four students annually in a three-year course". My area of responsibility had been defined as the developing of this training school. This involved the erection of buildings as much as the preparation of course material and the selection and training of the students.

The first major building of the school complex was nearing completion by April 1969. Much equipment had been bought in Kampala, Uganda. Slate blackboards had been acquired in Nairobi, Kenya. Chairs and desks, tables and cupboards, window and blackboard frames were being made by local carpenters. The building was to be dedicated to the Lord's use at the annual meeting of the Board of Directors (a rather fancy name for the humble group of missionaries and African church elders who met each year to pray and plan for the following year's activities of the medical centre, as part of the overall programme of church evangelism). The students had been working hard to prepare an anthem for the occasion. After the service, they were planning to serve a feast in the evening to all the workmen who had put up the building.

Unexpectedly, we heard that the day of the board's meeting had had to be moved forward by three weeks, due to unforeseen circumstances. We seemed to be miles away from being ready. Could we possibly accomplish all that remained to be done in just one week? Almost frantically we set to, in an all-out effort to beat the clock. For that week, classes started half an hour earlier each morning; the breakfast break was halved; the midday luncheon break was shortened by an hour; the football was confiscated; and everyone put to work from two to six to help the workmen complete the task. Local carpenters were urged to produce chairs as fast as they could. As soon as these arrived, in batches of ten, students sandpapered them and others varnished them. We just prayed that the varnish would be dry before the board members sat on the chairs!

Two students claimed to know something of painting, so were dispatched with two brushes and a one-gallon tin of white hard gloss paint, to tackle the window, door, and blackboard frames in each room of the school. Others helped to clear brick rubble, sweep paths, dig a garden around the newly-erected flagpole, and plant canna lillies which to our joy, because of the tropical climate, were actually flowering by Saturday!

Moving around inspecting all the different areas of work, I went in search of the painters to see how they were faring. They were not in the first classroom, which surprised me. When I did not find them in the second room, I became suspicious. I looked at the woodwork around the door, which had not noticeably changed since I last saw it. I touched it gingerly. There was a sort of brown, sticky "goo" ... I moved quickly across to the library. There they were, chatting away, brushes in and out of the paint pot, up and down the woodwork, totally unconscious that they were making no impression. The window frames looked just as before. I strode across to them and looked into the paint pot.

There was a solid mass of white matter, under a very thin remaining layer of rapidly disappearing linseed oil. The pot had not been stirred.

There was no point in being annoyed. It was probably my own fault, in assuming that they knew what to do and giving no instructions. One precious gallon of paint was wasted, as at that time we had no spare paint thinner. That paint was so precious. It seems ridiculous now, looking back from a distance, but everything was so hard to come by in those difficult days. We had waited literally months for the delivery of twelve gallon cans of paint. When they had arrived, three had already been stolen. Now another was wasted. I had to fight down a rising tide of frustrated irritation as I fetched another new can of paint.

I demonstrated the art of stirring. Hard work, right down to the bottom of the can, till all that was solid was stirred into the diluting oil, to become one consistency. It changed colour. It would not go so far now, but it would achieve the purpose for which it was designed. I left the two students, duly mollified, I thought, painting away with renewed vigour. Some half hour later, I suddenly realized that I had failed to explain that the paint would need stirring every so often until the job was completed. I hurried back to the two boys, only to find that, sure enough, the paint and oil were separating and the white losing its whiteness. I stirred, explained, and left them to it.

The next morning, being at heart a teacher, I gave the morning Bible study on the subject of "stirring" – how we as Christians need to let God stir us, right down to the bottom of our innermost beings. Paul had said: *"I put thee in remembrance that thou stir up the gift of God, which is in thee ..."* (2 Tim. 1:6), and I wanted to help each student to ask God to stir him deeply. We needed to be stirred until there was no separation left between solid and liquid, between secular and spiritual, weekdays and Sundays. Our lives needed to be of one consistency, through and through, ready to do the task for which we were created. This stirring would need to be continued daily until the task was completed. At the close of our Bible study, one of the students prayed in French, the government language, rather haltingly,

"Go ahead, God, stir me. I don't care what it costs ..." Then there was a long pause, before he burst out, in his mother tongue, "I do care what it costs, I care a lot, but stir me all the same, God!"

How my mind snapped back to Keswick, over twenty years before. That was the prayer of my heart then, and has been ever since.

"Stir me, dear God, to live for you in the very fullest sense, by the faith of Your dear Son, our Saviour Jesus Christ. Stir me, that I may step out of the apathy and indifference and lethargy that seek to overwhelm our modern society, in self-sufficiency and self-complacency. Stir me to move out into the exciting realm of faith, to see Jesus Christ at work through me in all the daily details of living. Give me the courage to believe and to act in faith."

This stirring of faith in my heart and life was as different from the stirrings of the "dares" of the days gone by as white from black; yet strangely, the one had moved to the other by the deliberate yielding to a new object of faith. Every part of my life was handed over, to be no longer a slave to Satan and sin, but rather to the mastery of Christ in His righteousness. I just knew that I now wanted to dare all to serve Him in the very highest sense of the word. It was not to prove my God able: it was no longer to prove myself able. It was just a deep longing, born in my heart by the Holy Spirit, to give Him all of which I was capable, my heart's devotion, my life's service, my will's loyalty.

STIR ME TO GIVE

Stir me, oh! stir me, Lord, I care not how
But stir my heart in passion for the world:
Stir me to give, to go, but most to pray:
Stir till the blood-red banner be unfurled
O'er lands that still in heathen darkness lie,
O'er deserts where no cross is lifted high.

1

STIR ME TO GIVE

Faith in receiving, and therefore in giving

> *"By faith Abel offered to God a better sacrifice than Cain ... God testifying about his gifts.*
>
> *"By faith Enoch was taken up ... he obtained the witness ... he was pleasing to God.*
>
> *"By faith Noah ... prepared an ark for the salvation of his household ... and became an heir of the righteousness which is according to faith"* (Heb. 11:4-5, 7).

As I began to live the life of faith (that is, exercising the sixth sense of faith) I slowly began to see and understand that everything in life relates to God. This living faith which creates a vital relationship between the Creator and each of His creatures is a free gift of God, available to all and to any who will accept it. This living faith is the most tremendous *fact* of the Christian way of life. It is, in itself, independent of feelings (though our appreciation of it frequently involves an emotional response). It cannot be earned or merited. It must be accepted as a gift, and then practised as a way of life. I have had to learn continuously to "live by faith," rather than by feelings.

This vital relationship to God has to be constantly asserted as a fact, resting on the historic events of Calvary and the empty tomb and independent of whether I happen to feel saved, or at peace, or in touch with God, or whether I happen to be discouraged, filled with doubts, or sensing personal unworthiness.

Thus, faith, as it takes over the direction of our wills, leads us into the "life of faith." As we learn to live by faith, by exercising that sixth sense which enables us to live in a constant relationship with God, so our actions will become the fruit of faith, bearing witness to its reality. One evidence of the fruit will be the growing exchange of the spirit of the world that demands to "get" for the Spirit of God who desires to "give." This spirit of *giving* is one of the most obvious fruits of faith. God's love manifests itself in giving:

For God so loved the world, that He gave ... (John 3:16),

The Son of God, who loved me, and delivered Himself up for me (Gal. 2:20),

whereas the overriding spirit of the world is one of getting.

"What do I get out of this?" is the natural man's immediate response to any new situation.

In the early days of our spiritual lives, there is often much to encourage and inspire our faith. This was certainly true for me personally – remarkable answers to prayer (too detailed and too numerous to be shrugged off as coincidences) and financial deliverances in times of need (sometimes accurate to the last penny and designated exactly, with no foreknowledge on the part of the donors). Initially we may think that our faith is increased by these miracles of God's giving. We feel this is so. Actually our faith, which is God's gift to us, cannot be increased; it is our realization of the fact of our relationship to God that grows.

Later, God may withhold some of the more startling, or more miraculous, manifestations of His giving, in order to establish us in the realization of our faith, independently of its fruit. At this time, our appreciation of the spirit of giving as the fruit of faith will gradually change from the childlike joy of receiving that which is given, to the adult joy of giving that which others may receive. Our faith, now firmly established, will be demonstrated in a spirit of self-giving that would have been inconceivable to us before the Spirit of God took over our lives.

This giving and receiving by faith may frequently manifest itself in what many call the miraculous. Though initially the believer in God too may see these events as miracles, yet slowly his understanding develops, and he comes to realize that these are the outcome to be expected of God's gift of faith. These miracles do encourage and stimulate faith, but ultimately we have to realize that they are not themselves proof of faith. If they were, then their absence would indicate a lack of faith. This is not necessarily so. Faith can exist without such miracles, though it is true to say that these miracles can only exist in the presence of faith.

This is certainly going to be a lifelong learning process for most of us. What can be seen and touched and measured and described often appears so real, while that which cannot be seen with human eye or felt with human hands, that which defies measurement or description, easily appears unreal.

As I began to see myself as I presume God saw me, I could hardly believe that even a great and mighty God could ever change *me* and fashion me into the likeness of His Son. I felt I knew so little of this life of faith; like Thomas, I always wanted to touch and see and handle and measure. Besides which, there was so much in me that I came to hate, things that I was ashamed of, thoughts that I would have done anything to be without. My motives often seemed all mixed up; selfishness and an attitude of "What do I get out of it?" seemed to pervade so much of my thinking. Could God really remould me to be like the Lord Jesus? That became the desire of my life; and God declares that all things that He brings into our lives are with the express purpose of doing just that! Could it be true?

And we know that God causes all things to work together for good to those who love God, who are called according to His purpose. For whom He foreknew, He also predestined to be conformed to the image of His Son ... (Rom. 8:28-29).

I also began to worry about what would happen if dark periods came, times of discouragement or even disillusionment. Would I be able to believe then? When I heard the testimonies of some missionaries and read of the experiences of Christians behind the Iron Curtain, I felt I could never be like them. Would I crack up under strains like theirs?

In the following years, there *were* times of darkness when I lost consciousness of the presence of God, when I felt I had no faith, and when I had no feeling of emotional enjoyment of the unseen and eternal. Doubts assailed, and the devil hinted that this life of faith was all a hoax.

There were times of bleak discouragement when nothing seemed to go right. Sometimes it was just the lack of material needs despite believing prayer, such as no roofing to complete the leprosarium dispensary before the wet season started, or the absence of an urgently needed antibiotic when the courier brought the monthly hospital order. Sometimes it was the apparent failure to make spiritual headway when students all seemed indifferent to the Bible teaching; when workmen were content with a shoddy standard inconsistent with our Christian testimony; or when in my heart I became irritable with God; grumbling at the long hours and heavy load of responsibility.

There *were* times of disillusionment. God had to break through the glamour surrounding the name *missionary* and make me "real." He had to show me myself as I really was, not as I pretended to be. I had to learn to accept myself as He accepted me, and therefore to accept my colleagues as He accepted them, but in the process, there were some dark months. There came the time when enthusiasm waned, and I came to realize that enthusiasm alone, apart from faith, was insufficient to complete the job. There came the time when the very vision dimmed, and God had to show me that even the vision alone, apart from faith, was insufficient to keep me going. There came the time when the highest aspirations seemed illusory, when companions and colleagues all seemed willing to settle for something less than the highest of which we had dreamed, that we had glimpsed, and that had fired us to throw away all else for its realization. It was as though cold water was poured all over the "flame of sacred love on the mean altar of my heart."

Could I go on believing? Would faith be extinguished? Could it be? Could it live, when all around seemed dying?

Will your anchor hold in the storms of life,
When the clouds unfold their wings of strife?

wrote Priscilla Owens.

✿✦✿✦✿✦✿

The conversion of Olga, the communist hockey captain during my first year at Cambridge University, was one of the first real answers to prayer that established my assurance of faith. I tried to bargain with God that if Olga were converted, and came into a full assurance of faith (this seemed about the most impossible thing for which I could ask!) then I would cease to doubt and vacillate and question the fact of faith. Olga was converted – truly, soundly converted – and my faith was established. When I later heard Olga's side of the story, how she had come to faith in God "because of your unshakeable assurance," I felt a little sheepish when I realized the graciousness of God in "pandering" to my childish demands. How good of God to work on our behalf despite each other!

I was to speak at a women's meeting one Sunday afternoon, a three-penny-ride away from Worldwide Evangelization Crusade (WEC) headquarters (about a three mile journey). I did not have three pence. Nor did I have the time available to walk. I kept my eyes on the gutter hopefully as I went to the nearest bus stop but no "stray" three penny pieces that day! The bus came, almost empty. I climbed the stairs to the upper deck and made my way to the very front seat. I felt bad about getting on without my fare but simply did not know what else to do. What would I say when the conductor eventually reached me and asked for the three pence? He would turn me off, and I would still have quite a long way to walk ... but less than the whole three miles, I reasoned, trying to calm my conscience that was clearly telling me that this was hardly an honourable way for a Christian to behave.

At the next bus stop, a crowd boarded the double-decker, and a lady sat down beside me. Eventually the conductor reached us. This lady passed him six pence, and asked for two three penny tickets, one of which she passed to me. Amazed, I just stared at it, then at her. I blurted out a thank you and then asked her *why* she had bought my ticket. Did she know me?

"No," she said, surprised. "I suppose I don't. I honestly don't know why I did it. I just know God told me to."

I looked at her closely, puzzled and a little awestruck. Suddenly she looked at me and added, "Are you by any chance our speaker for this afternoon's meeting?" and she mentioned the hall to which she was going.

In a very small voice I humbly acknowledged that I was. "That must be why God prompted me to buy your ticket!" she concluded with a lovely smile.

Yes, God was concerned about even the smallest details though He did not need me to sink to methods of deception and fraud to help Him achieve His purpose!

Other lessons had to be learned at the same time. I was travelling daily twelve miles to a hospital in West London from Crystal Palace, as a fifth-year medical student. There was a spell when I could not pay the needed train fare, and so was forced to cycle there and back daily. Then one day the front tyre burst, and I did not have money available to buy a new one. I tried patching it, but after two hopelessly frustrating days of effort I gave up and walked to the hospital. For three days, I set off at six o'clock to be on time for the nine o'clock ward rounds. After the last lecture, at six in the evening I walked home to supper at nine. On Saturday morning, in my pigeon hole in the letter rack, there was an envelope with my name typed on the outside and a five shilling book of stamps inside.

Thrilled, l went to the office and exchanged the book for five one-shilling pieces. Hurrying to the local shops, I bought a new tyre for my bicycle and with the change, a new inner tube. I used up all of the precious five-shilling gift. The afternoon soon saw the tube and tyre fitted and the bicycle ready to take me to the hospital on Monday morning.

Sunday was our monthly day of prayer at mission headquarters, and I joined with staff and candidates for the morning worship service. A thank offering was accepted as part of our worship, but I passed the plate by, having nothing to put in. At lunchtime, our British home director drew my attention to this and asked why I had not given a thank offering. He eyed me quizzically.

Colouring, I muttered that I had nothing to give, vaguely ashamed, with a sense of failure. Everyone else had enough faith to receive from God provision of their needs plus that which could be given away to others.

"But you *did* have something to give," he replied.

Annoyed and embarrassed, I denied this.

"But, Helen," he persisted, "you received five shillings yesterday in the office. Why did you not give the Lord His share? At least six pence belonged to Him by right" (five shillings equalled sixty pence, the tithe of which would have been six pence).

"But," I exploded, "I used the whole five shillings to repair my bicycle for work!" Again, there was a vague sense of shame or guilt or failure, I wasn't quite sure which; I felt his eyes boring into me, as though he could read my thoughts. *I could have done without the inner tube probably,* an honest voice inside was reasoning.

"Helen," Mr Grubb spoke quietly and kindly, "if you had given God His share *first*, He would have seen that you had all you needed."

I could hardly believe him or accept what seemed a harsh "rule of life," and yet that was probably the beginning for me of learning the blessing of putting God first in everything. Cash tithing became a lifetime habit, partly in obedience to scriptural teaching, partly as a private agreement of love between myself and God.

✧✦✧✦✧✦✧

My acceptance into the family of WEC was another milestone of faith for me. I knew, without any doubt or hesitation, that the staff were a spiritual group of men and women in close touch with God. If I was unfit to be a member of their family, if they sensed that I was not truly called to be a missionary, if they could not believe to see God change me into the image of His Son, I knew they would tell me. I knew that I was not worthy; I had no illusions there. They accepted me – not without a battle, maybe, but nevertheless they did accept me! – and my faith was further established that I *was* in the will of God for my life. Being accepted into the family was far more convincing to me as part of the life of faith, than any mere receiving of finance for specific needs without having made the latter known.

This latter aspect of the life of faith became for me, as it were, the tangible, external sign of invisible, inward grace. There were always financial needs, as for example, the weekly contribution for board and lodging, and it was always with a sense of exhilaration that one saw these weekly needs met. Sometimes an anonymous gift would arrive in the letter rack, or an envelope might be pressed into one's hand at the end of a meeting. Sometimes one knew the donor, other times not. Sometimes the needed gift came to one directly, at other times someone else might say that he had received double his needs and that God had prompted him to give to meet my needs also. Whatever the means used, God supplied.

When the time came for me to go to Belgium for eight months for language and medical studies, again God showed Himself faithful in providing the fare, the fees, and the weekly sum for board and lodging. It did not come all at once, but it came. I learned to trust Him, and, knowing that He would not fail, I did not need to panic if deliverance were delayed until the day it was needed! It was never late and did not have to be early.

The following year, even greater sums were needed for buying personal and medical equipment and the fare out to the Belgian Congo (Zaire of today). There was basic peace of heart, knowing that God would supply all that was necessary as He had promised:

My God shall supply all your needs according to His riches in glory in Christ Jesus (Phil. 4:19).

Faith was not really greatly stretched. Certain problems came to the forefront at that time, in understanding the principle of faith involved in obtaining financial deliverance. Was it right to help by dropping a hint of the need or by selling some unnecessary article? Was it right to expect from certain sources or to go to a meeting hopefully to give testimony, knowing that that church had given two hundred pounds a little while previously to another candidate? Was it right to "pray" about the needs every day till the provision was realized, knowing that God already knew and had heard the prayer the first time?

I *did* sell my medical textbooks, realizing about ten pounds – and then regretted it throughout the next twelve years of isolated practice when I could have done with every possible reference aid. I tried to sell my violin, but I was only offered five pounds for it, and I knew it was worth a great deal more; throughout the next twelve years I never regretted having it with me in Congo, for the joy it gave me and for the help it was in leading church worship. The people whom the Lord used to provide the means were all wide awake to the needs and sensitive to His prompting; they did not need me to tell them! In fact, the giving was sometimes so accurate to the specific need that one was tempted to wonder who *had* told them.

I went to one meeting, our mission's annual rally in an area of the United Kingdom where there was a reputation for extremely generous giving every year. Certainly in the back of my mind I felt this could well supply most of the money needed for my fare out to Africa. I received nothing. It was a salutary lesson to me. There was a very generous offering that was all sent to WEC headquarters for use in the leprosy and medical section of our work overseas, but God saw fit not to channel any to me that I might keep my eyes on Him and not on particular possible donors.

I remember the following week, going to another part of the country and there being asked to speak at a small, humble gathering. I was taken out to tea afterwards, and as the result of a quiet conversation, a gracious lady, recently widowed, gave me *all* of her doctor husband's instruments. It was a tremendous gift. I was humbled and somewhat overwhelmed by the loving trust she placed in me to use it all to the glory of God. Our small hospital at Nebobongo used that doctor's surgical instruments and medical equipment for the next twelve years.

God reminded me to keep my eyes on Him; He knew the sources He wanted to tap for all the needed supplies. I had no need for anxiety.

From the earliest days, for myself, I did not feel free to pray repeatedly for specific needs. Thus, when once the travel agents had told me what my fare would be, I laid the matter before the Lord and then practically forgot about it. Over many years, He has not allowed me to worry about the financial aspects of things. There have been other things that I have worried about, but somehow it was never hard to trust Him to supply all that was needed, in His own perfect time, where money was concerned. When big projects were involved, I used to ask Him to send me ten per cent of the needed total as a token of His good pleasure. Then I would step out in faith, believing that He would provide the remaining ninety per cent as it became needed. If the ten per cent did not materialize, I would question whether it was His will to move forward in the proposed action. When we started the reconstruction after the rebellion in 1966, at Nyankunde, our builder gave me an estimate of $15,000 for the classroom-library complex for the nurses' training school. Within three months, quite unexpectedly, we received $1,500 from an American government fund to aid self-help development programmes, which confirmed and underlined my confidence that the project was His, and that I could trust Him to complete it. He did. It took two and a half years, from the initial submission of drawings to the opening of the new buildings, but we never once fell behind in payments for labour or goods. To God be all the glory!

☼✦☼✦☼✦☼

Sometimes the way He provided was almost shattering in its exactitude, and I marvelled at those who had been so in touch with God that they had given *exactly* what He wanted given, at the very moment that He wanted it given – not that one should marvel at the perfect stirring of the Holy Spirit in the minds of believers. Presumably one should expect this as the normal, rather than see it as the exceptional. One day at the end of my first year in Congo, exhausted by the noise and heat in the busy polyclinic, I had slipped over to my home for a mid-morning break. I just felt that if I could have ten minutes' quiet to think straight, I could face the rest of the day better. On the veranda of my home stood an African man with his little wife, carrying a baby, and a two-year-old toddler clutching his hand. I did not want to see anyone just then and had to stifle back a rising feeling of annoyance. We went through the usual courtesies, and then he went on just standing. I was forced to ask him what he wanted.

"Work," he replied immediately.

With a relieved sigh, I explained that I did not employ people; I pointed to a house on the far side of the village where another missionary lived, who might be able to help him.

"No," he said, somewhat stubbornly. "I was sent to *you* to get work."

Puzzled, I asked what sort of work he wanted.

"I'm a cook," he replied quickly, adding, "I've been cooking for missionaries for eighteen years." (Fortunately he did *not* say that he had been cooking missionaries for eighteen years!)

"Why have you left your last employer, then?" I asked cautiously. If he had a reputation for burning the cakes, I was not keen to employ him!

Silently, looking straight at me, he rolled up the left sleeve of his shirt, and there at the top of his arm was the mark of leprosy.

Oh, no, Lord! I ejaculated in my heart. It was not that I was afraid of leprosy. I honestly was not. But this would mean another clinic squeezed in every week into my already over-full timetable. We would have to have a separate building, separate equipment, and medicines. In those days, public opinion was such that I could not treat leprosy patients in the general outpatient department. God should have known that I was already working nearly eighteen hours a day, utterly stretched. It was really unfair of Him to expect any more of me ... and similar thoughts grumbled on in my mind. However, to argue with God about treating leprosy patients is a waste of time; they appear to be among His special favourites!

Well, Lord, I said, *I can hardly have him in my home cooking for me. Whatever would my mother think if she heard that a leprosy patient was handling my food?*

So I tried in vain each avenue of escape from the situation. I suspect God's answer to me was that my mother did not need to know! So Aunzo came into my home as my cook. Together we built a small home for him and his wife and two little boys, behind my own home. We put up a small, one-roomed mud-and-thatch building to serve as clinic for the leprosy patients, just behind the newly finished men's ward at our small hospital. We sent off to Stanleyville (Kisangani of today), 350 miles to the southwest, for the needed medicines, bandages, and equipment.

Eventually the box of supplies arrived. Together, Aunzo and I opened it. He excitedly drew out the large bottle with ten thousand tablets of the new Dapsone drug that had just replaced the painful injections of Chaulmoogra oil in the treatment of leprosy. I picked up the bill – 4,320 Belgian Congo francs (in 1954, worth about thirty pounds, fifty pence). Somewhat caustically perhaps, I reminded God that I had not fifty pence available for paying the bill, let alone thirty pounds – and as He, Almighty God, had led me to start this particular clinic for the treatment of leprosy patients, I was sure that He would pay the bill, which I thereupon slipped into my Bible.

The end of the month came. Mission rules demanded that all bills be paid by the end of each month; no debts are allowed. There was *no* money available to meet this bill of thirty pounds, fifty pence. None. No fund from which I could borrow. I felt cornered. Why had God not provided? Such a sum would be nothing to Him, the price of one cow perhaps; but it was a fortune to me, three or four months' allowance in those days. I went to work that Saturday morning, the first of the new month, with a sense of grievance against God.

As I returned home at lunch time, Aunzo encouraged me to hurry, saying there was a brown envelope waiting for me. Another missionary had sent it across, apologizing that he had received it in his mail the previous day and had not noticed that it was addressed to me – from our field leader's office. Aunzo and I opened it together. I shook out the money, which he carefully piled and laboriously counted. I pulled out the statement. The total, in the bottom right-hand corner, came to 4,800 Belgian Congo francs. A quick mental calculation showed the tithe at 480 francs, leaving exactly 4,320 francs.

This total was made up of three gifts, from an unknown couple in North America, from two prayer partners in Northern Ireland, and from a Girl Crusaders' Union class in southeast England. The North American gift had been on the way some four months, transferred from our Philadelphia office to the London office, from London to Brussels, Brussels to Leopoldville (Kinshasa), and finally upcountry from Leopoldville to Paulis (Isiro). Every transfer involved a certain percentage cost. At the end, the three gifts had arrived together to make the exact sum needed, *and* two of the gifts were designated: "for your leprosy work" – and I did not have a leprosy work when the money was actually given! He knew, and He stirred hearts to give.

On other occasions, material goods were given rather than cash – but equally, the *right* goods at the *right* time. One night, I had worked hard to help a mother in the labour ward, but despite all we could do, she died, leaving us with a tiny premature baby and a crying two-year-old daughter. We would have difficulty in keeping the baby alive, as we had no incubator (we had no electricity to run an incubator!) and no special feeding facilities. Despite living on the equator, nights were often chilly, with treacherous draughts. One pupil midwife went for the box we used for such babies and the cotton wool they were wrapped in. Another went to stoke up the fire and fill a hot water bottle. She came back shortly, in distress, to tell me that, in filling the bottle, it had burst. Rubber perishes easily in tropical climates.

"And it is our last hot water bottle!" she exclaimed.

As in the West, it is no good crying over spilled milk, so in Central Africa it might be considered no good crying over burst hot water bottles. They do not grow on trees, and there are no drugstores down forest pathways.

"All right," I said. "Put the baby as near the fire as you safely can; sleep between the baby and the door to keep it free from draughts. Your job is to keep that baby warm."

The following noon, I went to have prayers with any of the orphanage children who chose to gather with me, as I did most days. I gave the youngsters various suggestions of things to pray about and told them about the tiny baby.

I explained our problem about keeping the baby warm enough, mentioning the burst hot water bottle. The baby could so easily die if it got chilled. I also told them of the two-year-old sister, crying because her mother had died.

During prayer time one ten-year-old girl, Ruth, prayed with the usual blunt conciseness of our African children.

"Please, God," she prayed, "send us a hot water bottle. It'll be no good tomorrow, God, as the baby'll be dead; so please send it this afternoon."

While I gasped inwardly at the audacity of the prayer, she added by way of corollary, "And, while You are about it, would You please send a dolly for the little girl, so she'll know You really love her?"

As often with the children's prayers, I was put on the spot. Could I honestly say, "Amen?" I just did not believe that God could do this. Oh, yes, I know that He can do everything. The Bible says so. But there are limits, aren't there? And I had some very big "buts." The only way God *could* answer this particular prayer would be by sending me a parcel from the homeland. I had been in Africa almost four years at that time, and I had never, never received a parcel from home; anyway, if anyone *did* send me a parcel, who would put in a hot water bottle? I lived on the equator!

Halfway through the afternoon, while I was teaching in the nurses' training school, a message was sent that there was a car at my front door. By the time I reached home, the car had gone, but there, on the veranda, was a large twenty-two-pound parcel, all done up with paper and string, and bearing U.K. stamps. I felt tears pricking my eyes. I could not open the parcel alone, so I sent for the orphanage children. Together we pulled off the string, carefully undoing each knot. We folded the paper, taking care not to tear it unduly. Excitement was mounting. Some thirty to forty pairs of eyes were focused on the large cardboard box.

From the top, I lifted out brightly coloured, knitted jerseys. Eyes sparkled as I gave them out. Then there were knitted bandages for the leprosy patients and the children looked a little bored! Then a large bar of soap – and the children were probably more bored! Then a box of mixed raisins and sultanas that would make a nice batch of buns for the weekend. Then, as I put my hand in again, I felt the … could it really be? I grasped it and pulled it out – yes, a brand-new, rubber, hot water bottle! I cried. I had not asked God to send it; I had not truly believed that He could.

Ruth was in the front row of the children. She rushed forward, crying out, "If God has sent the bottle, He must have sent the dolly too!"

Rummaging down to the bottom of the box, she pulled out the small, beautifully dressed dolly. Her eyes shone! She had never doubted.

Looking up at me, she asked: "Can I go over with you, Mummy, and give this dolly to that little girl, so she'll know that Jesus really loves her?"

That parcel had been on the way for five whole months. Packed up by my old GCU class, the leader had heard and obeyed God's prompting to send a hot water bottle, even to the equator, and one of the girls had put in a dolly for an African child – five months before in answer to the believing prayer of a ten-year-old, to bring it "that afternoon." Can God still perform miracles? Is He the same yesterday, today, and forever – in Israel, Africa, and anywhere else where He finds living faith? Indeed He can and is!

Then there were the Epsom salts. And on another occasion, the soap. And yet again, the very specific antidote needed for a certain type of food poisoning. There are so many exciting examples that leave one almost breathless as one remembers them all, and make it quite impossible to shrug off, as a casual coincidence, God's omniscience and omnipotence.

One morning as I started the ward rounds, a student nurse came to me with a report from the assistant in charge in the pharmacy.

"Please, doctor," he said, "Nengepeta asks that you write no orders for Epsom salts. We have emptied the barrel – there is none left."

That was a blow. We used Epsom salts extensively, not only as a purgative after treating a patient for intestinal parasites, but also as a cleansing agent for the terrible, external, tropical ulcers. My mind raced ahead, first trying to consider what we actually had in stock that I could use as an alternative, and then estimating when any further supplies might possibly reach us. We were so dependent on someone's happening to be going to the great city three hundred and fifty miles southwest, with room in their truck to bring us some supplies on the return journey who also happened to be someone trustworthy and with a good memory. (The others could so conveniently mislay or forget the order, yet still present us with a bill for it!)

The day wore on. Supplies of other drugs were also dangerously low. Would it be necessary for me to go myself to Stanleyville? If I did, how would they manage at the hospital while I was away? Would our ancient van make the journey there and back? All the time, I was planning and arranging and thinking over problems that often seemed insoluble, as well as outwardly carrying out a full programme.

I came back to my home for a cup of coffee at about four o'clock after teaching for a couple of hours in the nurses' school. There on the veranda was a wooden cask. I glanced at it, surprised. There was no apparent label anywhere, just my surname painted on the outside. I tried to swing it around, to look for a label on the reverse side, but it proved to be too heavy for me. I used both hands to shift it, realizing that it was about 100 pounds.

What was it? How had it got there? Not really concerned yet, and only vaguely interested, I went in for coffee. Aunzo brought it to me, as he heard me come in, at the same moment as my Alsatian friend, Trixie, came bounding in to me. I asked Aunzo about the cask out on the veranda.

"What cask?" he asked, puzzled, moving toward the veranda to see for himself. "I've no idea. I've been here all afternoon, and no one knocked or called. I can't understand how it could have come. Surely if a car had come into the drive, I would have heard it. And if by any chance I hadn't, Trixie would certainly have barked and called my attention to any visitor!"

We never did discover how it came, or where it came from, or who sent it. One thing only was certain when it was prised open: it *was* 100 pounds of Epsom salts!

The supply of soap was much the same. We had placed an order at the local palm oil factory for ten boxes, each of 240 pieces of white fat soap, made from the palm oil residue. This was a regular monthly order. Then we had heard that the factory was not working that month, due to some broken machinery. They were having to wait for delivery of new parts. We had been to the stores ten miles south, and to another four miles west, to buy soap, but they had none to spare, as their supplies came from the same factory. With our workmen, their wives, and families; student auxiliaries, their wives, and families; patients and their relatives; some eighty children in the orphanage; and over three hundred leprosy patients in our care-centre; as well as the regular work of a one-hundred-bed hospital with two to three hundred outpatients daily, it was not unusual to use one hundred bars of soap each day. It was hard to conceive everyday life continuing without such a basic commodity. Scrubbing floors and washing bandages and linen for the operation room alone was dependent on soap. Decent patient care and running a children's orphanage automatically needed soap. Whatever would happen without any?

On Saturday I drove fifteen miles along a forest road, in our three-quarter-ton pickup van, to buy plantain bananas for the family for the coming week's rations. As I returned, I stopped at every village, possibly eight or nine in all, buying the large heads of ripening fruit. At each stop, I hauled out of the van a fairly heavy weighing machine, which was then suspended from a convenient branch of a tree, to start our buying and selling session. Chair and table were also pulled from the van. After I had selected the best of what was offered, everything was piled back into the van, and we drove on to the next stop. So during the five hours of work, the van was opened and closed many times, and much went in and out, but always I was there, supervising and checking, choosing and paying, loading and driving.

When we reached home, shortly after noon, I drove straight to our evangelist's house to unload the plantains, where he was waiting to distribute the weekly rations to all members of the family. As we pulled out the heads of plantains, one after another, ten boxes of soap came into view, covering the floor of the van under the bananas. Who had loaded them in, how, and where, we never discovered – but God had met our need for another month.

Just before the rebellion in 1964, a six-ton truck drove into our hospital compound one day with over one ton of cartons and boxes of medical supplies, and one ton of blankets, bandages, and sheeting for the hospital. These had been unexpectedly sent to us by one of the large international relief agencies, and we were very grateful. That gratitude was, however, a little tinged with discouragement, as the consignment contained *no* urgently-needed antibiotics, antimalarials or analgesics, *no* routine medicines for coughs, intestinal worms, malnutrition, or anaemia, but rather, large quantities of hypotensives and anticoagulants (which we hardly ever needed) plus further quantities of unknown tablets, injections, and intravenous therapies, with labels in foreign languages, often in scripts unintelligible to me, with no accompanying list or clue to help identify them.

One such item consisted of two boxes, each of twenty-four quarter-litre bottles, prepared for intravenous therapy. I took one bottle home with me that evening, after sorting and stacking everything else, to work patiently and systematically over the label for some clue to the drug's identity and potential. Eventually I decided that it was a specific antidote for a rare type of food poisoning, where sufferers would have difficulty in breathing. Wearily I labelled the two boxes in Swahili and pushed them to the back of the top shelf in the pharmacy, "relegated to decay." Food poisoning is exceedingly rare among our tribal people.

Later the *same* week I was called urgently from morning prayers to the hospital. Two women, each clutching a one-year-old baby, were sitting there. The babies, twins, were in convulsions with great respiratory distress. As I arrived, one twin gasped its last breath and died. The other, despite every valiant effort, died twenty minutes later. Already, another group of four had arrived at the clinic, two fellows in their late teens, and a married couple of about thirty, all staggering in with racing pulse, great difficulty in breathing, breaking into a cold sweat with very low blood pressure. Two of them vomited violently as I went across to them. Student nurses of their tribe tried to glean some sort of history, and a horrifying picture unfolded. The mother of the twins, in the midst of the tragic wailing of tribal custom, suddenly had a violent epileptiform convulsion, foaming at the mouth, and unable to get a breath. Two more patients staggered in, one of whom collapsed and died in front of our eyes before we could do anything.

All came from one village, five miles to the east. There had been a wedding and feasting the previous evening. More people had come than were expected, and late in the evening, the womenfolk had gone out and gathered wild yams to add to the feast.

Wild yams? Oh, no, surely they couldn't have! They all knew so well the danger involved.

They said that by about two in the morning the first ones started to be ill. Some were vomiting, others just complained of chest pains and difficulty with breathing. All became distressed, and suffered a great paralyzing weakness. The whole community was smitten. None were exempt. None could help another. The few least ill had staggered to us in the first light of dawn.

Quickly we mobilized a team of able-bodied men, to prepare makeshift stretchers, and to race to the village to bring the patients to us. Several had already died; some died on their way to us; others died on arrival. Meanwhile, we hastily prepared a new building that we had just erected, the future women's and babies' ward, sweeping the floor clear of builders' rubble, spreading raffia mats, searching out every available blanket. I told the students to prepare bandage slings from the rafters, over every mat, for setting up intravenous drips. The pharmacy students were told to work flat out, preparing every available drip bottle with saline solution. The operation room team were told to sterilize all the rubber tubing and needles they could find, for drip sets. And I went and prayerfully took down the two boxes, containing forty-eight bottles, of a specific antidote for food poisoning. I dared not stop to reason about it, or to fear I had made a mistake in interpreting the label. I was just awed that God had provided for our need, the very week of that extraordinary situation.

As patients were carried in and laid on the mats, I moved from one to another, setting up drips. It seemed endless, all through the day. Many were deeply shocked, and it was almost impossible to find a vein. Some were obviously dying, and there was little or nothing I could do to help. Others seemed less ill and might pull through with warmth and stimulants. The rest, as soon as a saline drip was running satisfactorily, were switched to a precious bottle of antidote. Throughout those twenty-four hours we prayed as we struggled, and God graciously heard and answered. Those forty-eight patients all recovered, as did another twenty or so less ill who had not received the special antidote. Over twenty others had died.

I honestly believe most, if not all, of those forty-eight would also have died if we had not received that lifesaving medicine that very week. God's ways are very wonderful.

❍✦❍✦❍✦❍

Yet in the very midst of all such amazing occurrences and miracles to stir and stimulate our faith in God, there were also many other occasions when things did not work out just so simply. There was the pigmy lady, brought in after three or four days of obstructed labour, for whom I performed my first ever Caesarean operation. I was scared, yes, and very conscious of ignorance and inexperience, but we had prayed earnestly and claimed the Lord's enabling. Everything went wrong that could go wrong, and on the ninth post-operative day she died. Had God not heard our prayers?

Throughout my twenty years in Africa, I was scared of surgery. I never got over this feeling, even though I became reasonably competent and experienced, at least at Caesarean sections and hernia repairs, setting of fractures and essential amputations, skin grafting for burn victims and relief of strangulated piles. I could no longer blame ignorance and inexperience for my fear. I prayed about this fear. I asked others to join me in praying that I would be delivered from the unreasonable degree of fear. Yet the fear remained. Did I not have the faith needed to receive the answer to the prayer?

When I asked God for money for a project, such as the purchase of a much-needed vehicle to act as ambulance; or the reroofing of the maternity compound with permanent materials to replace the badly-leaking thatch; or the monthly supply of medicines and equipment for the hospital and salaries for workmen and nurses, He always answered – clearly and undeniably sometimes "yes," often "wait," rarely "no." But this reply was visible and tangible. Monthly needs were met regularly for twelve years at Nebobongo – He never failed. In the fifties, the needs rose from £10 a month to about £50 a month. In the sixties, they continued rising to about £100 a month before the rebellion and possibly £250 a month following the rebellion. In the seventies, the needs had rocketed to nearer £1,250-£1,500 a month – and still the Lord faithfully, regularly supplied. Oh, there were test months, when the supply did not materialize until the very last minute, but we were never forced into debt or late in paying wages. Some of the money, in fact over the years an ever-increasing proportion of the money, came in locally from patients paying for medical care; but there was always, and still is, a considerable subsidized balance, paid by God through free-will offerings from the homelands – and His portion was always ready on time!

Larger projects, as for the building of the training school at Nyankunde, that needed nearly £50,000 before completion, over a ten-year period, all came in. Sometimes one hardly knew how or from where, just that the books balanced and the bills were paid.

As I claimed by faith these supplies of our financial needs and saw the Lord regularly answering that prayer, why could I not also trust Him to deliver me from my burden of fear? During the rebellion this became an acute problem. Fear became an overwhelming dominant force that tried to stifle faith. It was an external, violent evil that oppressed the spirit. I cried out to God for deliverance, yet fear persisted.

But then I saw that through fear I was reaching out to touch God minute by minute in a new way. Right in the midst of the crushing torment of fear, I had peace, unbelievable peace, peace that passes understanding. God was greater than the fear. Fear was a physical fact, emanating from the evil presence of the enemy, but in it and through it peace triumphed. That triumph probably was greater even than an expulsion of fear would have been. It was God manifesting Himself as "more than conqueror." He did answer my prayer but not in the way I had expected!

So, I realized, with surgery. Though the fear persisted in my own acknowledgement of lack of training and consequent insecurity, nevertheless He gave me daily the courage needed at each call to go through with the allotted task, to tackle the emergency whatever it might be. And over and over again, He proved Himself capable as a surgeon, as in every other area of need!

A friend wrote to me in May 1964 reminding me that "courage is not the absence of fear, but going through with God in the face of fear." Again God was meeting my need, giving the strength and courage which by faith I was receiving, even without realizing it.

Similarly, we longed so much to see spiritual fruit in the lives of our students and pupils. By faith we received from God that fruit, the result of daily praying and daily preaching and, as He enabled us, being a daily living example among them. We really longed for this more than anything else. It was not just because this was what missionaries ought to want or ought to say they wanted. No, it was a real deep burden of heart, that each young life that came to us for medical training might catch such a vision of the Lord Jesus Christ as to become honestly new creations, in whom "the old has gone: the new has come." The very purpose of our being there, the purpose of our training programme, was that each student might be caught up in the purposes of God as an "ambassador for Christ," to go out from us to serve his fellow men in the love of Christ. Our teaching programme did not merely include Bible training, but rather it centred on their spiritual training, that each one should *"grow up in all aspects into Him, who is the head, even Christ"* (Eph. 4:15).

What went wrong? I look back on a long list of disappointments (perhaps one should use a much stronger word). Only one of the first group of six students has gone on in his spiritual life; only one of the second group of three is with us in church membership today. I only know of five from the next three years' entrants. Of the two hundred students who have passed through our training programme since we moved to Nyankunde and an inter-mission leadership following the civil war of the sixties, probably some one hundred and forty are making no present effort to live according to their declared Christian faith. Although many of these are serving their country as medical auxiliaries in the state programme, one has to be honest in recognizing the unbelievable corruption that permeates this programme and in which our graduates, as others, become fully involved – stealing and selling medicines and equipment on the black market; treating patients only on receiving exorbitant bribes; drinking heavily and being unavailable when needed for night emergencies; careless and indifferent to hygienic standards and the care of the ill.

How can this be? Where did we fail them? They were faithfully taught, not only to have high ethical standards in medicine, but also, by the enabling of the Holy Spirit, to "be like the Lord Jesus Christ" in all aspects of character and daily living, growing up into Him in all things. They answered well in all examinations; they practised well throughout their years of training and probation; they appeared to me to be real and sincere in their understanding of, and desire for, the "deep things of God." Yet when the crash came and they hurled abuse at us and scornfully repudiated us, we heard by the local grapevine that it had all been going on right under our very eyes, even in training school. One senior student, going out every Sunday teaching spiritual truths in a local village, on the very day that he received his medical diploma, went off to get drunk. Returning at two in the morning (having been missed at ten when there was a surgical emergency) he openly laughed at us, declaring he had no more need to "keep up the pretence"; he had gained his diploma, thank you, and was now off. The following week we heard that he had been living for two years in adultery with a girl in the village where he preached each Sunday. My heart was crushed.

Another, accused of adultery by a woman patient in the hospital, was having his "affair" investigated by a local disciplinary board when he simultaneously was accused of murder in a neighbouring village. He was taken to prison, initially to save his life from the villagers who would have lynched him in their anger. Under fear of death, he poured out to me a story of unbelievable rottenness during the three years he had spent as a student in our training school. He could not number the women with whom he had lived, nor even the children he had fathered. He drank heavily and spent much time in local drug and drink dens. He had lied all the way through his college course. He stole medicines from the hospital and sold them on the black market. There seemed no end to the list of things which he confessed. At last he was released from prison, acquitted of the charge of murder,

on condition that I arranged *at once* for his transport back
to his own tribal area, 350 miles to the northwest. He
went back home, at my expense, I thought repentant
and humbled at the greatness of God's mercy and grace,
seeking forgiveness for all he had confessed to me. For
two years, he worked under the watchful eye of pastor
and church elders, loved, cared for, and nurtured in the
ways of truth. He was then allowed back into medical
service for a trial period when suddenly he left. He was
heard of shortly afterward, working for a plantation in
their administrative service – right back in the ways of his
past life, indulging every imaginable passion, without the
slightest pretence of restraint.

These are two. There are others, oh, so many others.
They have been more prayed over than those who have
"gone straight," who have rejoiced our hearts. Is it not
possible to receive from God's hand grace for their lives,
the power to lift them out of all the greed and self-seeking
and dirt that surrounded them, that they might live clean,
upright lives? If God could do this for us, surely He could
do it for them?

One great problem was stealing medicines or equipment
or money. They did not always see it as stealing. They
"borrowed" from the kitty, putting in an I.O.U. note
– but then they failed to honour the note. This trouble
was so deep-rooted that they themselves pleaded with
us to "hold the bag." We were voted onto otherwise all-
African committees just to act as treasurer. They did not
trust themselves: they did not trust each other. But if God
could take away all desire to steal from my heart, surely
the same God could do the same thing for them?

Could I not exercise faith in prayer that they might
receive this power from God? I realize that ultimately,

each student must be personally responsible before God as to how he or she responds to the offer of salvation and to the promise of power through the Holy Spirit to live godly lives; yet was the extent of our failure to see such response in their hearts and lives a measure of some lack on our part? Was it because I was unwilling to be stirred to *give* something that God wanted of me?

There was the tragic story of the midwives in 1961. After the granting of independence to the country in June 1960, basic administrative leadership at our Nebobongo medical centre had been handed to an African committee. Naomi, a twenty-year-old trained midwife, brought up in our own orphanage and local schools, was the obvious choice of leader for the maternity complex, even though she lacked the spiritual maturity of Damaris Banakiamonu, an older woman with a deep love for God, but who had only just qualified as a midwife. The latter was co-opted onto the committee for her spiritual contribution, but Naomi was officially in charge.

Almost at once, trouble started. The group of four or five younger, qualified auxiliary midwives, under Naomi's leadership, took the law into their own hands and determined to run things their way. They objected to all advice or any restraint, and the missionaries found real difficulty in fitting into the new scheme. Standards began to fall. We tried desperately to refrain from criticisms and to keep in the background. Flagrant breaking of rules began to take place. Men were seen in the girls' compound at other than visiting hours. Damaris became silent and grieved, working steadily and uncomplainingly, but obviously without her usual buoyancy and joy.

Then one night, the seventh of March 1961, the trouble boiled over. Florence, my missionary colleague, and

I were praying together in my home, when we became conscious of a strange noise. Uncertain and a little fearful, we had crossed to the maternity compound to investigate the source of the noise. Damaris and the evangelist's wife, Taadi, attracted by the same noise, joined us. We found the midwives and pupils, led by Naomi, surrounded by a crowd of cheering and clapping men and women from the nearby villages, leading a pagan festival, beating rhythmically on empty gasoline drums and singing lewd songs to well-known hymn tunes.

I prayed earnestly that God would fill me with a willingness to give myself more wholly, more un-reservedly, for those flouting authority.

We the leadership, national and foreigner, except for Naomi, spent the night in prayer, "our hearts heavy with grief, a deep sense of failure and disappointment mingled with righteous indignation and horror" that all this had been perpetrated by those whom we trusted, those responsible for preaching the gospel daily in their wards and clinics.

Naomi and five other midwives were dismissed. We started the work again.

They appeared mildly amused by our embarrassment, and somewhat sarcastic at our concern, both for themselves and also for the work and witness. Within five months we learned that most of them were expecting illegitimate babies. Our hearts felt broken. How had we failed them? Was our judgment at fault? At what point had we ceased to be able to get through to them? We had had *faith* in God that they, by His indwelling power, could be trusted and enabled to lead despite their great lack of training and experience. Our faith seemed not to be justified. Had God failed? That was unthinkable; He would not then be

God, almighty and sovereign. Was it not God's will that these lives be given over to Him, indwelled by Him, and caused to triumph over temptation, as He was doing for us? That was inconceivable. We knew it was God's will. What was the apparent missing link that made it possible to have faith for people as much as for material supplies?

God kept saying to me, by one means and another, through my daily Bible reading and through letters from friends at home: *love* them – love them more. "Love" seemed to mean "give" – *give* yourself for them.

For God so loved the world, that He gave His only begotten Son (John 3:16).

Greater love has no one than this, that one lay down his life for his friends (John 15:13).

I prayed: "Stir me, oh! stir me, Lord ... to give ..." To give, I had and was. I meant it, yet I balked at the involvement. Would I really give them twenty-four hours of every day, seven days a week? I remember a day, many years later, when I had thought this lesson learned, but had to realize that it was not yet part of me. I was called at 1:30 a.m. to help in the operating room; it was a slightly complicated Caesarean section, and I stayed with the mother after surgery for an hour or so to see that she was all right. It was nearly daybreak when I reached home and hardly worth going back to bed, so I made myself a cup of coffee, and had a time of prayer and Bible reading. Down to school by 6:25, I was irritated by the students "wandering in" from 6:35 to 6:45, and I spoke to them sharply about this growing slackness where punctuality was concerned. This started us off on the wrong note for the whole day. At eight o'clock, I was given a list of "missing tools" by my works foreman, and spent the half-hour breakfast break going over it with him. At 11:15 a.m., a note was passed into the classroom where I was teaching. I could almost hear the students hold their breath as they knew "the doctor does not like to be disturbed" when lecturing It was from the foreman, asking me to go at once, urgently, to the local marketplace, some two and a half miles away, where there had been a minor accident involving the college truck.

There was no vehicle available just then, so I borrowed a bicycle and cycled the switchback route. The uphills always seemed steeper whichever way I was travelling. The midday tropical sun poured down. There was an ugly crowd at the market, gathered in two tribal groups, shouting and threatening each other, and our foreman, the driver of the college truck, was in the middle. Moving in quietly, listening, seeking to pacify, hearing both sides, weighing up the scanty evidence amidst the host of irrelevancies, being jostled and pushed around, all in the growing noise and heat, was quite alarming, but eventually we extricated ourselves and the truck and made for home. It was mid-afternoon. We were hot, hungry and somewhat exhausted. I had missed two classes, and it would be very hard to make them up in our tight schedule. In the evening we had a school staff meeting, and there was a particular matter that I wanted them to agree to quickly. It all seemed so clear and logical to me. It should only have taken five minutes to mention and for them to accept the proposition.

But, no! Others wanted endless details and reasons and explanations. I was almost cross-examined over the affair, and I could feel my irritation rising. Why could they not just say yes? Surely if I proposed something, that should be sufficient. As school principal, could they not trust my judgment? All this endless discussion was such a waste of time. How pigheaded could they be?

And they doubtless thought that I was very high-handed and obstinate. Why would I not share properly? Had I something to hide? Was the affair not quite so straightforward as I was trying to present? So they reasoned that they had better be careful and weigh it up thoroughly before being forced into a blind agreement.

Eventually I climbed the hill, homeward bound, shortly after ten. I was very, very tired and somewhat ashamed. Somehow, the day seemed to have gone all wrong. It certainly had not been "Christ living in me" most of the time, but rather a very dominant "I" ruling the roost. I went to the kitchen and lit the stove to heat some milk. Then I went out of the back door to draw a bucket of water for a bath, from a forty-gallon drum heating over the dying embers of the day's fire.

As I came in again there was a sudden, sharp knocking at the front door.

"Oh, no, thank you! Nothing more today!" I muttered under my breath, and turned the storm lantern very low and stood absolutely still, so that the would-be visitor would think there was no one in and go away.

It did not work. In a moment, he knocked again, loudly and persistently.

I turned out the stove, put down the bucket, and went to the front door. I just had time to pray that God would take over. I knew that "I" was too tired to face any more, and I would let God down hopelessly if I tried.

Out on the veranda, in the dark, stood a senior student in obvious distress. I invited him in and lit the lamps. After making us each a steaming mug of hot chocolate, I sat down to listen. Slowly, haltingly, he began. With a little judicious prompting and questioning, he began to pour out a tale of unhappiness, resentfulness, failure, and loneliness – all well concealed during the two or three years he had been with us, under a cover of quiet correctness and apparent obedience. In the early hours of the morning, on our knees together, he sought the Lord's mercy in forgiveness and knew the ineffable joy of being born again by the Spirit of God.

> *Being justified as a gift by His grace through the redemption which is in Christ Jesus* (Rom. 3:24).

How nearly I had failed that lad! Obviously I am telling of an occasion when I did *not* fail. I dread to think of the many other times when I simply was not "available to God" for the outworking of His purposes. That particular day I had given God twenty-one hours, and I had considered that I had a right to the other three for sleep. God was trying to teach me that He wanted all my *time* (as well as my money, and my ambitions, and all else that made up my life). And, of course, when the lad left me, I was exhilarated. All sense of weariness had fallen away! I was still physically tired and slept well until the morning, but God had poured in the strength needed for the task that He wanted to do.

✧✦✧✦✧✦✧

As we pray God to stir us to *give*, we must be prepared to have faith to give Him *all*, unreservedly, not measuring the apparent cost. Sometimes as I talk like this at a public meeting, people challenge me.

"How," they ask, "can you ask young people to throw away their lives, to go to serve God and their fellowmen, in a foreign land, after all you have suffered yourself? Is that fair of you? Are you working on their emotions, while hiding from them the horrific realities and dangers that you know exist?"

And I could add, "And parents, when I challenge you to *give* your children for missionary service anywhere in the world, remember that I do so in the full glare of the stark reality of the massacre of thirteen missionaries and their children in Rhodesia by the guerrillas in June 1978. There is nowhere that this could not happen again, nowhere that can be called 'safe' in our modern, sin-torn world of uprisings and rebellions, coups and counter-coups."

Yes, God challenges us to have faith to give Him all, to trust Him with all we have and are, and to watch Him work out the consequences. But even as I thought I was learning the lesson and passing it on to others, I could see areas in my life where I failed completely. We were challenged to have a weekly meeting of the school staff for *prayer*. We agreed that even if there was no urgent business for discussion, we could always pray. We all knew that we needed more time for corporate prayer – for claiming together, by faith, all that we longed for in the lives of our students as well as of ourselves.

But we did not do it. Or rather we did not keep it up. We started well. We meant well. But it became crowded out with other more pressing busyness. The daily routine of preparation classes, marking books, supervising practical sessions; the other committees that claimed each other evening of the week; the pile of unanswered letters that demanded attention; the quiet excuse that I needed one evening a week off for my own affairs – always there seemed some valid excuse why the prayer meeting should wait until next week.

And so in 1958 we lost Bakiogomu; in 1962, Bumu-kumu; in 1964, Kuriye; in 1968, Njonjo; in 1970, Songoli; in 1972, Bakanganibyuteli; and so one might go on. Each was a promising young graduate; each fell to the pressures of the enemy in one direction or another, tempted by money and material gain, or sexual indulgence, or drink, or stealing and selling drugs on the black market. To these could be added a host of other names, of students who had to be dismissed before they ever qualified – usually for drunkenness, or adultery, or stealing, that had gone on until they got themselves inextricably involved in a net of vice and deceit. If we had been willing to give ourselves more, could we have exercised faith on behalf of these and seen them rescued and established?

God asked me to give not only time but service. I had prayed, "Stir me, oh! stir me, Lord ... to give ... *all* that I have and am, to Thee." I meant it, or at least I thought I meant it. Then He tested me on the reality of my desire. When I grumbled at all the manual labour I was asked to do, which seemed to me to prevent my being a good doctor for the population I served, I accepted His rebuke. There was the time when I had to come up from the brick kiln to do an emergency operation, and my sore hands, bleeding from handling bricks, smarted under the nail brush and antiseptic alcohol of the scrubbing up procedure. When I complained about it, the church elders showed me that my time spent with the workmen down at the kiln had broken down barriers and built up bridges of meaningful communication in a way that my medical skills had, till then, failed to do. As a result I was willing then to give that sort of service to God, as well as what I thought of as more specifically missionary service.

Yes, but it only went so far. God had to spell it out to me over and over again, in every different situation. I seemed unable to learn the basic principle. The life that is lived by faith in the Son of God is a life that has given up all rights on all levels, to its own ways and choices, accepting that the Son rules in every part on all occasions. When He asked me to give up my supposed right to boss, to run the show, to make all the decisions, I failed to see what He was getting at, and we ended up with rows among the team members, even over such petty things as the correct time and the price of eggs. I was certainly not exercising faith to live in happiness and harmony with my fellow missionaries and colleagues, simply because I would not give to God my right to be the boss. I was living an "I" dominated life, rather than a Christ-indwelled life. I had to learn to *give up* the "I."

Similarly, my pride in "my" work – my students, my hospital, my choir, my football team – was a stumbling block to a true walk of faith in God. This pride led to a continuous desire for visible results. I wanted to measure what "I" was achieving. My faith needed to touch in order to believe, as Thomas with the nail prints in the hands of his risen Lord and Saviour.

> *Jesus said to him "Because you have seen Me, have you believed? Blessed are they who did not see, and yet believed"* (John 20:29).

It was hard to learn the lesson. To walk by faith and not by sight had to become a living fact of relationship where the reality of the unseen was more real than the appearance of visible results. Seeking results is often a not-very-subtle means used to prove the reality of one's faith, when in actual fact it only shows the existence of doubts in one's mind. Results *per se* are no proof of the existence of faith, any more than the lack of visible results are the proof of the absence of faith.

Looking back, I can indeed see how He was at work – breaking, melting, moulding – even though at the time the way was often obscure. I can now remember with joy the fact that, on the morning of the day when I was finally taken captive by the guerrilla soldiers and had to leave Nebobongo after twelve years of service, I had taught in the six-thirty morning Bible study from the fourth chapter of the prophet Malachi, the last chapter of the Old Testament Scriptures. It was the culmination of four years' teaching, during which time we had studied together the whole of the Old Testament writings. Most of that last morning's congregation are still in full-time Christian service. The almost unnoticed daily sowing of the seed, giving of oneself to God morning by morning, and living in a faith relationship to Him as one ministered to others, was to bring a wonderful harvest over the years. The preaching and teaching ministry during subsequent years, in hospital and maternity wards, among workmen and in surrounding villages, by John Mandadima and Damaris Banakiamonu, by David Bebesi and Bernard Basuana, who were fed and nurtured during those four years of Bible teaching before the rebellion, can never be measured. The numbers who have found the Lord as their Saviour as an indirect result can never be counted.

Through the years God has to move us from the thought that faith is merely a force that operates to *take* things wanted, until we realize that faith is a fact in itself, the fact of knowing God in His omnipotent sovereignty, immaterial of things obtained or otherwise.

There is of course tremendous scriptural warrant for the encouragement of faith by miracles. In the first sign that the Lord Jesus Christ performed at Cana in Galilee when He turned the water into wine, we read that *"He manifested His glory, and His disciples believed in Him;"* (John 2:11). Faith was brought to birth by seeing the miracle performed.

The second miraculous sign that Jesus performed, having come from Judea to Galilee, was the healing of the dying son of a royal official. As a result, as "the father knew that" the moment of his son's recovery *"was at that hour in which Jesus said to him: 'Your son lives;' he himself believed, and his whole household"* (John 4:53-54).

Throughout John's gospel, eight special miraculous signs are recorded *"that you may believe that Jesus is the Christ, the Son of God, and that believing you may have life in His name"* (John 20:31).

We could recount endless miraculous events in recent years throughout the ranks of our mission, to stir us up in faith, as when one candidate, returning from London on a crowded subway, with her passport at last bearing the precious entry visa to the land to which she had been called to serve, had her wallet snatched. As she stepped from the train onto the busy teeming platform, she realized her loss. Turning back toward the train, she saw the already-closing doors reopened, and the train remained stationary, contrary to all expectations. She jumped back into the car and nervously raised her voice to announce her loss and to plead that whoever had taken the wallet (including all the precious documents for her departure to the mission field that very week) would be constrained to return it to her.

And in amazed silence – doubtless to the majority who witnessed the scene, in utter incredulity that anything could result from such a plea in such circumstances – the wallet was handed to her. She left the train, the doors closed, and the train departed. God had vindicated her faith.

On another occasion, a missionary family was returning to the West from a Middle-Eastern country by Land Rover. As they approached the long 400 mile drive across the desert, many warned them that it was impassable. Steady, unrelenting rain was turning the whole ill-defined route into a mud path. Not even a Land Rover would achieve the long climb up over the mountains and the hazardous drop on the northern side. They had no possible alternative. Prayerfully, in faith, they moved off into the desert. And God prepared a way for them. To the right, it was dark with thunder and torrential rain. To the left, it was dark with thunder and torrential rain. Behind them, as they drove northward, darkness closed in, with thunder and torrential rain. But before them, throughout the whole journey, was a shining pathway, continuously dried by a north-easterly wind, with sunlight by day and moonlight by night. Truly God had honoured that family's faith and made a way before them.

Books have been written on the wonderful supply of financial and physical needs for the children's home at Arbroath, the training college in Glasgow, the conference centre at Kilcreggan. Books have been written of how God has stepped in over and over again in crisis situations, in answer to the faith of His missionary servants in all our far-flung fields of service. Books have been written of how fields have been opened, churches planted and established, educational and medical projects built up and developed in many parts of the world involving tremendous financial responsibilities for properties and personnel, for equipment and transport. Over and over again, at the word of faith, we have been greatly encouraged to see God manifest His sovereign power on our behalf, and miracles achieved to His eternal glory, as He has supplied all that was needed.

Yet, faith is *not* dependent on the seeing of miracles; faith is not even proved by the performing of miracles. Faith must be a relationship with our sovereign God, independent of miracles. In the gospels, we read of the death of Lazarus, when presumably Christ could have healed him. Agreed that four days later our Lord raised him from the dead, but Christ said that his *death* was to reveal God's glory. In the early church, Stephen died by stoning, though God could have prevented this; James the brother of John was put to death with the sword, though Peter was miraculously rescued from the same prison. Paul ultimately died in Rome under the cruel persecution of the caesar of the day, though John survived his exile on Patmos under similar persecution and came home to die of old age. The faith of members of the early church was not based on deliverances and miracles only, though doubtless these helped greatly to encourage and enrich their faith, as we can see in Hebrews 11:32-40, where we read of those who "shut the mouths of lions, quenched the power of fire, escaped the edge of the sword" and of women who "received back their dead by resurrection." However, "others were tortured, not accepting their release." There were those who "experienced mockings and scourgings, yes, also chains and imprisonment. They were stoned, they were sawn in two ... they were put to death with the sword." Some lived, some died. Some were rescued, others were not. Some escaped, others "went about in sheepskins, in goatskins, being destitute, afflicted, ill-treated ... wandering in deserts and mountains and caves and holes in the ground."

And these "gained approval through their faith," the faith by which they gave themselves wholly in obedience to God, not counting the cost, the faith of God living in them and enabling them, as Paul wrote of them, as their spiritual goal:

> *I have been crucified with Christ; and it is no longer I who live, but Christ lives in me; and the life which I now live in the flesh I live by faith in the Son of God, who loved me, and delivered Himself up for me* (Gal. 2:20).

In like manner, we also came to understand God's sovereignty in His dealings with us during the Congo uprising of 1964. He chose to rescue some of us from imminent danger of death. He chose to allow others to die and go to be with Him in glory. Equally, God has chosen to heal some from humanly-called terminal disease, whereas He has chosen to allow others, with equal faith and peace of heart, to continue the natural course of the disease until they died and passed into His Presence.

The faith of each one of the heroes mentioned in chapter eleven of the letter to the Hebrews was fixed in God. Likewise the faith of each of my fellow missionaries in the Congo uprising of the sixties was fixed in God. So also was the faith of the many Christian friends and members of our families, who prayed constantly and believingly for our deliverance. We were all delivered, some for further living here on earth, some for future living in God's presence in heaven. We know, without question, or doubt, that God acted on behalf of each of us for our good, according to His perfect plan and purpose. Our faith in Him, and in His power to deliver us was not shaken, nor weakened, by the different ways He chose to act in that deliverance, be it to life, or through death, to eternal life. Faith is not dependent on God's visible *acts*, but on the indisputable *fact* of His relationship to us.

Stir me to go

Stir me, oh! stir me, Lord, till all my heart
Is filled with strong compassion for these souls:
Till Thy compelling Word drives me to pray:
Till Thy constraining Love reach to the poles
Far north and south, in burning deep desire –
Till east and west are caught in love's great fire.

2

STIR ME TO GO

Faith in guidance, and therefore in going

"By faith Abraham, when he was called, obeyed by going out to a place which he was to receive for an inheritance; and he went out, not knowing where he was going....

"By faith Abraham, when he was tested, offered up Isaac; and he who had received the promises was offering up his only begotten son ... [Abraham] considered that God is able to raise men even from the dead; from which he also received him back as a type" (Heb. 11:8, 17, 19).

One evening, coming home from church, I suddenly drove into dense fog. My headlights glared back at me, reflected from the impenetrable blanket. The sticky droplets froze like an opaque sheet across the windshield. I could see nothing.

Braking hard, I pulled a side window open. Poking my head out, a wave of relief swept over me as a tiny bright light shone up from the road. As I crept forward, it blinked out and another took its place some yards ahead. From one cat's eye to the next, I crawled up the winding hill road to the junction with the main road. For a moment, I nearly panicked as there were no cat's eyes to guide me across the road. An approaching car, turning the corner to my right, shone its headlights down the crest of the road as the driver also crept from one small reflector to the next. He stopped to read the signpost, his arm stretched out of the window, holding a flashlight. I used his headlights to creep forward and turn into the main road, before he turned off to the left, and once more I started forward following the precious eyes. Now and again the fog lifted briefly, and I could see ten or twelve eyes and moved forward more confidently. Then as I approached a corner, my searching headlights found no eye until I slowly turned to follow the curve of the road. It was a cautious, rather frightening journey, yet while I could see the eyes, I could travel with a degree of confidence. Step by step, yard by yard, I followed just the short distance I could see, one eye after another, without demanding to see a long way ahead.

Suddenly, I was clear of fog. The dark night seemed full of starlight, and in the distance, the lights of a neighbouring town sparkled in an intensified clarity after the murk of the fogbound hills. I moved forward easily as my headlights shone powerfully down the length of the road to the next corner, and I was hardly aware of the little sparkling cat's eyes as I sped past them.

This is a parable of how God guides us along the rough and the smooth parts of life's way. All He demands is step-by-step obedience to the *next* stage as He shows it, without waiting to see a long way ahead.

But what are God's "cat's eyes" on our journey through life, that we may place our faith in them and move forward with confidence? How do I find out where God wants me, and for how long He wants me there? By faith, can I really be so sure that I can either step out and go, or else, with equal assurance refuse to be pressurized into going, knowing I should say no?

Often the actual *where* of going is not very important, however contrary this statement is to popular belief. Two other things are much more fundamental and therefore of far greater importance.

First, we must be completely certain that God *has* a plan for our lives. God does not begin looking for a place for us to fit in, when we start praying for guidance. God's plan is already complete. Each of us is created to fit into that plan:

> *For we are His workmanship, created in Christ Jesus for good works, which God prepared beforehand, that we should walk in them* (Eph. 2:10).

When we ask God to guide us, we are asking to be shown the job He has already "prepared in advance for us to do." We are simply stating a willingness now to go His way for us, instead of continuing in our own way (Isa. 53:6). It is by the faith of the Son of God indwelling me that I am assured that God has a place for me. It is by this same faith that I grow to realize that outside of God's prepared place, there is no ultimate satisfaction or peace of heart for me, and so I desire to be led into His will for my life.

Secondly, I must become willing to be one hundred per cent available to God for whatever He has planned for me. No holding back. No saying: "Yes, Lord, except ... ," or "God, I'll go anywhere You send me, as long as, please, You do not ask me to go to ... , or to leave such-and-such, or to work with so-and-so." There must be a willingness for unconditional surrender of obedience to His will, if I am to have assurance of being centred in that will.

As with the pot of paint, I must be stirred right down to the bottom, thoroughly and truly, until no solid matter remains separated from the diluent, till all becomes one consistency, one colour. When the paint is so stirred, it is ready to be applied. If I will allow God all rights to my life, to stir me until He sees I am ready to be applied, I can trust God then, in His perfect timing, to know where He wants to apply me. God does not need to tell us ahead of time. Until we are stirred, we are not ready for application.

Take for example the urge that enters a Christian's heart toward the beckoning needs of full-time service, overseas or at home. The first part of the stirring for that person may well be to show the need of application to present studies. As the pressure of that urge continues and cannot be subdued or silenced, though as yet with no sense of specific direction, the next step in preparation may well be to Bible school or missionary training or a cross-cultural adaptation course. Many a student has received confirmation or assurance of the final destination for service during these training days. Some simply become more deeply committed to the privilege of being God's co-labourer, anywhere He sends them, with no specific geographic leading.

Certain burdens come to the forefront at this stage, as for the Muslim world, or the immigrant and refugee peoples, or the social injustices of intolerable poverty or unimaginable hunger. In accepting this burden from the Lord, the next step becomes clear, to learn more of the facts underlying the need, and further training in one direction or another is obviously the next right step. So step by step, in obedience to light given, sometimes almost imperceptibly, we move from "cat's eye" to "cat's eye" in God's plan for our lives.

Sometimes there may be a sudden clearing, and we see far ahead and leap forward with joy and anticipation, and a great sense of assurance of God's direction. Sometimes the way seems darker or foggier than usual, and we must trust to each next reflector to light us on our way. Driving day or night, we cannot see around the next corner until we turn it! However far ahead our headlights reveal the road, it is always only to the next bend. As we approach the bend, our view ahead gets progressively shorter, until suddenly there is not one remaining "cat's eye" to guide us until we turn – and there they are again! Guidance is given for as far as God wants to show us at any given moment.

There are problems; of course there are. Equally there are rules to help us to know where to look for guiding signs and how to recognize them, just as with the car driver. The rules and illustrations as to how to tackle the problems are all supplied in the Highway Code. We are told of red reflectors on the outside road edges, to warn us of danger if we stray across them. There are green reflectors to our near side when a junction occurs to warn us to be aware of the possibility of approaching traffic. The regular white reflectors are up the centre of the road, and our dipped headlights will hold them in view if we are travelling straight and safely. Oncoming traffic can blind us if we let our eyes be caught in the glare of their headlights; this is best avoided by concentrating our vision on the cat's eyes in the centre of the road or along the nearside shoulder. Overtaking traffic can disconcert us or discourage us, throwing powerful beams far farther ahead down the road than our own rather feeble lamps reveal. We must keep our minds on our own course and speed, by watching steadily in our own beams, even if gaining a moment's encouragement by seeing far ahead as the other one sweeps by us.

So God cares for us as we travel the road mapped out by Him, for our life's journey. The rules are plain for us to follow in obedience. As we obey each step of the way, so will the problems be resolved, and the next stretch become clear to us. The directions God gives us, that we may know Him and read His map for us, do not include a blueprint for omniscience, that we may know what is around the next corner before we reach it, but rather a blueprint for intelligent obedience that will enable us to reach and turn the next corner safely whatever we meet around it. We are not advised to ask God *why* the road curves, but to ask God's wisdom to follow the curves carefully and without accident. When we meet a parked car, it is not of interest to us to know *why* it is parked there, but it is of paramount importance to us to know the rules as to how to pass it, that we may not put ourselves or other road users in unnecessary danger, by passing on the wrong side.

So what is God's highway code? Where are all these directions to be found? Surely in His written Word, the Bible. I pray that God may stir up my faith in His Word as *the* compelling force to direct and control my life. His standards are clearly set forth, and His commands with regard to keeping those standards are equally explicit. The more frequently, the more regularly, and the more prayerfully that I read the Bible, the more sure I shall be of the path that He has planned for me. God teaches me clearly through the example of the life of His Son, our Lord Jesus Christ, recorded in the gospels. By His life and His teaching, Christ reveals to us the character of God. Paul, Peter and John in their epistles, under the inspiration of the Holy Spirit, take this teaching and apply it to our lives, that thereby we may become like Him – *"conformed to the image of his Son"* (Rom. 8:29). The Old Testament abounds with signposts to help us – examples to follow, warnings to heed, failures to shun, precepts to obey.

This last point is probably the cornerstone. If as we read and study the Word, we seek grace to obey God's revealed precepts, we *shall* find guidance; that is, we shall discover that we are being guided day by day, possibly often without actually realizing it. So often when I am fumbling about, seeking guidance, feeling that all is dark, and unable to see any familiar landmarks, not even the glimmer of a "cat's eye," the reason for my fog is disobedience to a clearly stated precept. For example, it is unrealistic to seek special guidance as to whether I should or should not do a certain action, when the action concerned is sinful according to scriptural standards. I do not have to seek guidance as to whether or not I should marry an unbeliever or date a married man, any more than whether or not I should falsify my income tax returns or lie to a customs officer. In each of these cases I need to ask for a spirit of obedience to God's commands, rather than for guidance as to my reactions. If indulged in, these would each be acts of disobedience. Not only do they not in themselves, therefore, pose a problem of guidance, but they may, if persisted in, even cause an absence of guidance. A realization of guidance is dependent on concurrent obedience to God's revealed will.

Perhaps, without stretching the analogy too far, this point can also be illustrated from the parable of the cat's eyes on the road. If, as a driver approaches a corner in the road, he fails to heed the absence of further eyes by slowing down, but rather by maintaining speed he leaves the road, he cannot blame the eyes (nor the absence of eyes) for his accident. Moreover, he cannot seek further eyes to rescue him from his predicament without first getting back onto the road! We must obey the light we have been given, step by step, if we want further guidance and help along the way.

I travelled that same road from church to my new home another evening, but this time there were no cat's eyes visible. Everything was carpeted with an inch or more of glistening snow! So what? My friend was travelling just ahead of me in her car, and she knew every inch of that hilly road like the back of her hand. All I had to do was to keep close enough to follow her bright red rear lights. As we approached a corner, the brake lights shone out a warning to me: as we came to a turning, the flickering yellow indicator light told me clearly to prepare to turn right or left. A glance upward at the sheer beauty of the snow-etched tracery of the branches of the arching trees nearly caused disaster, as I did not notice the brake lights ahead, and almost rammed the leading car. I realized that I must concentrate only on the lights ahead and enjoy only that amount of the surrounding beauty that those lights revealed without turning my eyes or thoughts from the road I was following.

On another occasion my friend and I had been together in her car returning from an evening meeting, when we drove into one of the worst fogs either of us had ever encountered. For two or three hundred yards we had crept forward, following the dimly seen rear lights of a car ahead of us. We had to remain very close indeed to the leading car, if we were not to lose him. Suddenly he was gone. A thick, impenetrable blanket of fog had sealed us in. With heads out of the windows on each side of the car, searching to see the white line of curb or crest we had crawled forward at less than walking speed, and then found ourselves with no white lines, no cat's eyes, no rear lights of a car ahead, and yet being followed by a line of other cars, relying on our rear lights as guides! A concrete post loomed out of the fog, within inches of the front bumper, and, as we braked, we prayed that the cars behind us would not pile up on us.

A face appeared at the window, as we tried to find courage to know how to begin again.

"Can I help you?" said a kindly fellow traveller.

He backed up the four following cars, one by one, and on foot guided us by flashlight into the correct lane of traffic, thanking us for leading the way, before returning to his own car. The procession continued forward gingerly, until suddenly we left the dense fog zone, and our headlights leaped forward into the clear night air once more.

Once in Africa, driving northeast from Kisangani on the long 350-mile journey to Isiro and Nebobongo, I found myself, in a small three-quarter-ton van, behind a huge, eight-ton truck. I tried to sound the horn, to tell him of my presence and encourage him to find a spot along the narrow winding shoulder where he could pull off and allow me to pass. The horn failed. Aggravated, I sat doggedly behind the truck, hoping at each bend in the road that he would catch a glimpse of me in his rear-view mirror and give me the right of way. But he was throwing up such a massive cloud of red dust as he churned forward, that it was impossible for him to see anything following him. Again and again I tried to attract his attention but all to no avail. An hour and a half later, some thirty miles or so along the road, dusk fell quickly, and I leaned forward to switch on my headlights. With horror I realized that "no horn" also meant "no lights!" The truck ahead lit up ... and for four hours, covering over one hundred miles, I drove forward in the lights of that truck. It was frightening. It was difficult. I dared not lose him or lag behind him. As he turned corners and I had still to reach the corner, the darkness seemed to engulf me. I could not stay too close in case he braked suddenly, or lost control and skidded, yet I must stay as close as I possibly could. Fortunately, we did not pass another vehicle, in either direction, during the whole of that crazy drive.

At last, nearing eleven o'clock, he drew up at a wayside rest area, and I gratefully drew in behind him. I was almost exhausted with the strain, but I was also exhilarated with the success! We had kept exactly equal pace throughout; we had followed him exactly all the way. I staggered out, went over to the driver, and thanked him for his (quite unconscious) leadership!

God's leadership is always conscious, and He never sets a pace that we cannot maintain. When the corners come, He is there waiting for us, to take us around safely. We must just stay close enough to see the guiding light continuously, or hear accurately the directions of the still small voice. Guidance is a very personal business. Basic rules are there for us all; the code book is to be studied by every traveller. However, the actual route and pace are decided separately for each individual. Following the one who has gone before (as it were, the car ahead) is fine if we know that it is heading for the same destination as we are, and if we are sure that the driver himself knows the way.

With God, we know that He knows the way we should take, and that He will make no mistake in guiding us to our true destination, But how can we be sure that we are following Him, obeying His direction, listening to His voice?

✿✦✿✦✿✦✿

I was gloriously certain of God's direction in my life to be a missionary. I had no doubt that the urge in my heart to train to be a medical missionary, to give my life to serve others in a foreign land, was an urge given by God. Everything I read in the Word seemed to underline it. It was all so clear to me, I could not truly understand those who did not feel the same urge. "Go and tell ..." "Go into all the world and preach ..." "You shall be My witnesses ... to the remotest part of the earth." It did not seem to matter where I read in the Word: verses leaped out of the page to confirm this calling to me. I could not get away from it. Speaker after speaker at Christian Union activities spoke of the joy and privilege of being His co-labourer and of the enormous need throughout the world for full-time missionaries. Why did others not hear as clearly as I did?

God beckoned me on. He did not seem to me to whisper. I felt He shouted His directions from every rooftop! Every Sunday sermon seemed to include a challenge. Every midweek meeting I went to, someone would add yet another comment about the needs and opportunities of service. The very air seemed to throb with the insistence of the command to go.

As the Father has sent me I also send you (John 20:21).

This was a triumphant promise of His accompanying presence, as one moved forward in His will.

And it was for life. How could it be less? "Love the Lord your God with *all* ..." – all time, all energy, all possessions. Christ Himself said that we could not be His disciples unless we were willing to renounce all. This must include all rights to set a time limit, to give a partial

97

obedience or limited commitment. Peter, when Christ called him to follow Him and to become a fisher of men, forsook *all* – his father and home, his boats and nets, even the miraculous catch of fish that he had just landed, that would have sold in the market for the price of a whole week's supplies. Must this call to missionary service not be for life? The interpretation of the whole trend of Scripture seemed so clear to me, and it was with joy that I moved forward, in obedience to the Holy Spirit's prompting, and offered my life for full-time missionary service.

Would that joy last? Would the certainty of being in the centre of God's will for my life continue when the going got rough? As a medical student I could see quite a long way down the road, and the cat's eyes gleamed brightly and unmistakably. Six years would pass before I was qualified, time to be filled with as much preliminary training for future service as possible: experience; Bible school; missionary training programme; language study; cultural adaptation; and then a lifetime of service as a preacher and a practitioner. In my imagination, I travelled around several corners ahead and was quite oblivious of the problems and hazards.

Early corners were negotiated fairly easily. When illness made it look unlikely that I would ever be accepted by a missionary society, God gave me confidence through a verse in my daily Bible reading:

> *Do not fear … My servant … whom I have chosen. For I will pour out water … My Spirit … My blessing* (Isa. 44:2-3).

When tutors advised me to give up medicine, and my own inclination echoed the advice, God halted me with a clear message at the weekly Bible study group from Nehemiah:

"I cannot come down …" (Neh. 6:3).

When seeking clarification as to where He wanted me to serve Him, three times in one week a small phrase of Scripture was brought to my attention – first seen on the tear-off calendar in the mission dining hall one Sunday morning; second sent in a letter by an old school friend who did not even know that I had been converted, her letter coming on the Wednesday morning; and on the third occasion used as the text at morning prayer on the Friday

Repair the damages (2 Kings 12:5 KJV).

On the last occasion, the leader used the phrase to underline our responsibility as a mission fellowship to provide a medical service for the national church in Congo, which we had helped to bring to birth and establish.

The following week, when I was given the right hand of fellowship by the leader of the Worldwide Evangelization Crusade, and was welcomed into family membership, he gave me a verse for my life's service:

Thou shalt be called, the repairer of the breach (Isa .58:12 KJV)

and any lingering fear or doubt, as that corner was negotiated, disappeared, as one more clear "cat's eye" shone out.

Years later, after a somewhat rough passage when everything seemed to be going wrong and I doubted if the Lord could ever use someone as hopeless as I, and I felt in a deep fog, uncertain of the next step, Pastor Ndugu spoke at the early morning prayer meeting from Ezekiel:

God said, "I searched for a man … who should … stand in the gap before Me …" (Ezek. 22:30).

In Swahili, the "man to stand in the gap" was the same word as the "repairer of the breach!" A cat's eye shone out of the gloom, and God guided me around another corner.

The day I left Ibambi, where I had worked for eighteen months under the leadership of senior missionaries with only very limited responsibilities, and went to Nebobongo to take over much fuller leadership responsibility in the village and church, as well as hospital work, that morning my daily Bible reading was in Exodus, chapter two, verses one to ten. Verse nine leaped out of the page and, seemed written just for me.

> *Take this child away and nurse him for me and I shall give you your wages.*

God promised to provide all that was needed for the accomplishment of the task He had called me to accept for Him. Clearly the promise had no time limit. The task seemed immense – to provide an adequate medical service for half a million people in one hundred thousand square miles of territory. Momentarily I could see a long way down the road. In imagination, I saw the training school for national medical auxiliaries, the regional hospitals, surrounding clinics, airstrips, and radios – a lifetime of service to turn the vision into reality, and I moved into the straight with renewed confidence.

The eighteen months of fighting in the civil war of the Simba uprising in the sixties wiped out all that had been achieved. A fog descended and blotted out all familiar landmarks. Would we ever be allowed to return? Had I been wrong to be so sure that it was for a lifetime? Was it realistic to start again, should the way open up, knowing that the uprising could break out again at any moment? Was it right to expect God's people to provide the huge finance that would be needed to recreate all that had been destroyed, with no possibility of protection from repeated destruction?

Had God not promised to provide the wages? Why now doubt?

Had He not called me to repair the breach? Why now hesitate?

He spoke again clearly through Isaiah 61:4-8 and promised to rebuild all that had been destroyed, and wipe out all that had caused shame. I went back again to Congo (now Zaire) with peace in God's leading. The weekend before we sailed, God spoke again to our hearts from Jeremiah 32:27, which posed the question facing us:

"Is anything too difficult for Me?" asked the Lord,

and in verse 17 came the ringing assurance:

"Ah, LORD God! ... Nothing is too difficult for thee."

Then, during the initial rehabilitation programme, amid the heartbreaking turmoil of destruction and faced with enormous financial and personnel needs, a new vision began to form in my heart and mind. Basically it was not new, but a development of the old – a growing realization of how the former vision could be translated into present reality.

To "repair the damages," in providing a medical service for the ever-growing population of the northeastern region of Zaire, needed a well-trained national team of medical and paramedical workers. Nebobongo school was one of a group of centres providing such training that had been virtually brought to a halt by the civil war. Could we not "repair the damages" better by amalgamating all the small schools that had existed previously into one central training institute, capable of higher standards, and able to use fuller teaching techniques, and supported by a larger hospital and a more efficient staff? My commonsense reasoning said a clear yes to the idea. Talking the plan over with others of like vision brought an immediate agreement. Sounding out the government involved more detailed planning as to just what we felt we could offer in a certain eight-year period; and they gave cautious approval. Choosing the location for the new project was overruled by embassy advice to the American missionaries involved.

Everything fitted. Was it God's will?

Certainly it would facilitate the fulfilment of His command to repair the breach; but God had sent me to Nebobongo to nurse the infant medical service there for Him. Nyankunde was 350 miles away, in an entirely different tribal and cultural setting. When I broached the subject of a possible change of location for me to the Nebobongo staff, national and foreigner, there was a reaction of unbelief that speedily changed to horrified opposition. It was useless to explain that eventually they would gain by the change, receiving better qualified national workers to fulfil the service; all they could see was immediate loss. Their one and only doctor was talking of leaving them. "A bird in the hand is worth two in the bush" is an old adage which my colleagues could understand only too well.

A letter came from the senior doctor of the team interested in creating a central hospital to serve the whole vast area, with a direct invitation to me to join them, and to be responsible for developing the new training school. Within the week, in my daily Bible reading, I came again to the verse in Exodus 2:

Take this child away and nurse him for me and I shall give you your wages.

To me God had spoken clearly and decisively. The first "baby" at Nebobongo was getting on its feet. There was a team of national workers, with the missionary nurses, able to maintain a reasonably good medical service, backed up by a flying doctor service from the newly proposed centre. Nyankunec clearly seemed the new "baby," just born, and certainly needing loving nursing care.

Nearly eight years later I was home in England. It appeared probable that my service in Africa was ended. My mother needed my companionship and help. Now how would I explain my "call to lifetime service?" How could I explain it to my own heart's peace and satisfaction, without a sense of guilt or failure? That God's call was for full-time obedience to His Word on a day-to-day basis, I could easily understand, but I had been so sure that He was sending me to Africa for life. I had testified publicly to this certainty. Now what?

That mother needed me was equally sure. God's Word stated my obligation to her, to love, honour, and care for her. I was happy to do so. I asked the Lord to seal the rightness of the decision by sending replacements to my task at Nyankunde within a year. In a wonderful and remarkable way He did so.

Nancy Houser, a Canadian medical student in Toronto, had spent three months of her fifth year of training at Nyankunde, staying with me in my home.

Philip Wood, a London surgeon, met Nancy at an international conference for Christian medical students and graduates.

They married; went to Belgium together to study for the diploma in tropical medicine and hygiene; spent four months at the British headquarters of the Worldwide Evangelization Crusade; and flew to Zaire, arriving at Nyankunde six weeks before I was due to leave. During those six weeks, we packed in an intensive course of language study, a tour of introductions, welcomes, and farewells in the area for which they would be medically responsible, and a detailed handing over of responsibilities in the training school.

I came home. God had clearly guided and sealed the guidance. Yet I was full of doubts. Had I merely used mother's need of me to escape from a task that had begun to overwhelm me, from a situation of nervous tension due to petty bureaucratic harassment that I could no longer tolerate? Was I trying to "manipulate" guidance to come up with a desired answer? Could I be sure it was God's voice, and not just my own plausible reasoning?

Mother died, in many ways unexpectedly, despite long years of pain and increasing physical limitations. Now I could return to Africa and so I wrote to various African colleagues. I needed a clear word of present-tense guidance from the Lord. Older missionary friends questioned this. "He called you out here for life; why do you need another word? Does God change His word?"

For the gifts and the calling of God are irrevocable (Rom. 11:29).

I found that I no longer wanted to go back. This was unbelievable to me! I had always loved Africa, and every furlough I had counted the days until I could return. After the rebellion, it had needed very little prayer to discover His will; I simply had to return. Africa was home. Her people were my family. I was homesick to be back with them. To me, life in Africa, despite all its difficulties and frustrations, was always preferable to life in the United Kingdom with its materialism and superficiality.

Now the urge to go back was no longer insistent. Was God bringing contentment to my heart that I might accept from Him redirection for service?

I embarked on a prolonged period of intensive deputation ministry for the Worldwide Evangelization Crusade. People came to meetings, people of all ages and from all types of church background. They listened, they were challenged, they responded, they came again and asked for more! God blessed the tours. Daily He gave strength and enabling, vision and sensitivity to particular needs.

It was not a job that I would have chosen. I feared that my colleagues would feel that it was a soft job, that I had opted out of the harder job of returning to the medical service in Zaire. Eventually, driven by my own guilt complex rather than any sense of divine guidance, I wrote a letter to the missionaries in Zaire, tentatively offering to go back. Nothing came of it. No one responded. It was as though I had never written. I felt rebuffed. I had been so sure that I was wanted, so sure that they would invite me to return at once. Instead of accepting God's guidance into my present sphere of service, I had sought to force God to change that guidance, or else to force my missionary colleagues to acknowledge His guidance in what I was already doing. I had tried to use my letter to Zaire, with its implied request to be invited to return to the overseas field work of our mission, as a "fleece" (as Gideon acted, in Judg. 6:36-40) . I had reasoned: "If God wants me back in Africa, the team will leap at my offer and unanimously say, 'Come': if God wants me to work in the English-speaking Western world, they will not say,

'Come.'" Perhaps I was only seeking corroboration of the guidance I believed that God had already given me. Whatever my reasoning, they said nothing; I felt hurt.

How inconsistent could I be? If God was "wetting my fleece," why was I not glad of His clear guidance? It was what I had asked for. Was it really no fleece at all, because I had been so sure that it would "remain dry," that is, that the field would leap at my request to return? Had the field (possibly unwittingly) shown that they accepted that God had guided me to stay at home at this time? If so, they had answered my prayer for an assurance of being in His will. Either the consequent silence to my letter was God's clear answer to my request for guidance, or else it was His quiet condemnation of the means I chose to seek that guidance. Either way, I was unhappy, and that is so often the result of placing fleeces to gain guidance. I have learned through the years that fleeces rarely work as a valid means of guidance. They can too easily be rigged, or else each fleece can lead to a series of secondary fleeces until the practice becomes ludicrous,

God *was* speaking to me, though I was slow to recognize His voice.

One way He spoke was by this silence from the field, another was the absence of an urge in my heart to return. Yet another way was through the churches and groups that I was visiting during my deputation tours. Church after church, group after group, wrote and invited me back for a second meeting, as they told me of blessing among their congregation from the ministry the Lord was graciously permitting through me. Young people were applying for Bible schools, older groups were gathering to pray together for missions in a way they had not been doing previously. Yet despite all this, I was afraid – afraid that

I was not hearing *His* voice, afraid I would miss His will, His best. I was afraid that I was allowing my common sense, my personal preference, to overrule. Had He not clearly called me into a lifetime service? Had He not clearly directed me to Nebobongo and to Nyankunde? Had He changed? Could He change?

I was still in full-time service, only the sphere had changed.

The "baby" at Nebobongo, and later at Nyankunde, was growing, walking, adolescent, moving toward independence. New directors had been raised up for their guidance and help. I appeared to be given a new "baby" to nurture, in making known the urgent needs of millions throughout the world, as yet unreached by the gospel of God's redeeming love, and the endless opportunities available, for those who would enter God's service with this one burning desire in their hearts, to make Christ known. The means to achieve this – meeting with people, staying with people, talking to and listening to people; studying magazines, reports, and statistics so as to have answers and challenges ready – all seemed to demand a stronger, more extroverted nature than mine.

I found myself back in Exodus 2 and the repeated command:

Take this child away and nurse him for me

and the clear accompanying promise:

and I shall give you your wages.

I weighed up all the arguments, a few "for" and many "against." The next day my reading was in Exodus, chapter 3, and the day following, chapter 4, telling of Moses' arguments against obeying God's clear directive. I was impressed by God's continued patience and His quiet persistent dealing with Moses, wiping out objections one by one. I felt ashamed of my unwillingness to believe and to accept His guidance. My major objection was: "What will others think?" with many variations on the theme. Besides, I was a bad traveller and a poor mixer. I was inwardly shy and found it difficult to relate quickly to each new situation.

I became ill and had to have major surgery. On the third day following surgery I asked a nurse to open my Bible at the marker and prop it up in front of me on the bed table. I asked God urgently for a clear and certain word of direction. Then I read the next chapter from where I had left off reading a few days previously. It was chapter 3 of the second book of Kings. As I reached verse 16, it leaped out at me, clearly as God's answer to my prayer, but I did not understand it.

Make this valley full of trenches.

I knew the context fairly well, having spoken on it on one occasion. The three combined armies of Israel, Judah and Edom, with their respective kings, had taken a six-day march south through the mountainous desert region encircling the south end of the Dead Sea, to approach the southern border of the territory of the Moabites, across the Arnon valley. They hoped to refill their water jars at the river, ready for an early morning attack on the unsuspecting tribesmen. One calculation had been at fault. It was the dry season, and, there was no river! Mutinous mutterings began to spread like a prairie fire among the restless, tired, thirsty soldiers.

The kings, almost desperate at the crisis that had developed, sought for a "prophet of God" to deliver them (despite having made no reference to God when they set out for this vindictive war). Against his own inclination, but in acknowledgement of the God-appointed king of Judah, Elisha had prayed for them and sought God's face for a word of direction.

"This is what the LORD *says," he told them. "Make this valley full of trenches."*

Hard, back-breaking work at the best of times, given the right tools for the job. Without these tools, in the heat of the dry season with no water to drink, it was a formidable task. "Digging trenches" was normally for latrines in an army camp and was considered to be detention duty for soldiers under discipline. With mutiny very near the surface, this seemed a wholly unreasonable demand. Yet ...

It was clear that if God should graciously send rain, trenches would be essential to capture it. The dry sandy river bed would hold nothing on its surface in this arid waste. Yet ...

The command was given. Possibly in defiance, perhaps in resignation, the soldiers complied. Each man dug his little trench. Soon the whole valley was filled with several thousand little ditches, together a veritable Suez canal! That night, with no sound of wind and no sight of rain, the trenches filled with water. Next morning, the parched troops and their packhorses gratefully, greedily quenched their thirst.

God did more, the over and above. Not only did He supply the army's needs, but also He overcame their enemy! The Moabites, looking down from the mountain to the north across the Arnon valley into the rising sun, saw the river bed as though filled with blood – red from the reflected morning glory. Presuming this to be the result of mutinous strife, the Moabites poured down into the valley in total disarray, unprepared for battle, merely to fall on the spoils. Immediately the Israelite Judean army rose up, in disciplined ranks, and fought back the enemy forces, inflicting enormous losses and winning an overwhelming decisive victory.

God said to me in my own immediate situation, "Make this valley full of trenches."

"But God, if a trench, why not a Suez Canal?" I countered. "Do what I ask," God commanded me, "little by little, trench by trench, and leave Me to work out the consequences."

The army was not trained to dig trenches and had not the right tools. It was hard and humiliating work. It seemed senseless and unrewarding. Could I step out in faith and believe Him and trust Him to work it out? It was to be in "this valley," where I presently found myself, in the midst of my own difficulties. It would involve me in a work for which I felt I was not trained or prepared or equipped. At least temporarily, it would exclude me from the work for which I felt I was trained and equipped.

"Get going now," God seemed to say to me. "Do not fear, or shrink, or hesitate, or argue. Don't try reasoning or explaining. Just obey."

Within the week, I was invited to go to a girls' summer camp to recuperate. Trench one.

Within one month, I was welcomed to go for one year to serve on the staff of our missionary training college. Trench two. During the first year, I had opportunity to speak at over one hundred meetings, telling of the needs of the world. Trench three. In fact each meeting appeared to be a separate trench, with opportunity and responsibility. As I kept moving on, it seemed that each trench behind me filled with the water of blessing, though I was rarely allowed to drink of this myself.

Meanwhile in Africa, God was blessing the new college directors at Nyankunde and, through them, the students in their care. He had allowed me to have some part in the ditch-digging process in the years of preparation to receive the blessing that He was now pouring upon them.

As I sought to continue in obedience, making my present "valley" full of ditches, God graciously wrought peace in my heart, and by faith, the realization that He had guided me into the sphere where He wanted me, however slow I had been to understand this.

☼✦☼✦☼✦☼

Each one of us needs to be stirred in our faith, to go wherever God would send us. This may be far or near. Usually it will simply be a moving forward in the obvious line of duty, with no "extra" word of guidance. God has promised to check us if we deviate from the way but not necessarily to applaud us if we remain constantly in the way.

> *And your ears will hear a word behind you, "This is the way, walk in it, whenever you turn to the right or to the left"* (Isa. 30:21).

On one occasion, someone was needed to drive from our village of Nyankunde across the mountain range of Central Africa to Kampala in Uganda, a 200 mile journey. We left at four-thirty in the morning and climbed the long, rough road up to the border post. Customs formalities took time, and we had to move our watches forward an hour as we crossed into a new time zone. Then the steep descent down the escarpment to the source of the Nile and the long, dusty drive across the Ugandan plateau, skirting the Murchison game reserve. Eventually we reached the northern tarmac highway from the capital and drove the last seventy miles fairly comfortably and considerably faster than the previous hundred-odd miles. After a bite of supper and a bath, tired out from driving all day, I fell into bed at about ten-thirty that evening.

Next morning, I left Kampala well before dawn, on the long journey home. Racing northward on the good high road, I was alone with nature. No one else was yet up or on the road. I watched the dawn break over the plains, enjoying the bird chorus, when suddenly I realized, with an unpleasant swerve, that I was dangerously near to falling asleep. Unable to throw off the waves of sleep, I decided that the only safe thing to do was to halt for a coffee break.

There was a clump of bushes some little way ahead, and I drew up there at the side of the deserted road. Getting out, I found myself face to face with an African! Quite honestly, I did not want to see an African just then; I did not want to see anyone, white or black. We went through the usual courtesies. He was speaking East African Swahili, and I, West, but we could make ourselves understood. After the courtesies he should have gone away; they always do, in their innate politeness. But he just stood there.

I asked him what he wanted. "Are you a sent one?" he queried.

Puzzled, I hesitated. That is doubtless the meaning of the word *missionary*.

"Well, yes," I assented, adding hastily, "but it depends – sent by whom and for what?"

"Are you a sent one, by the great God, to tell me of the thing called Jesus?"

It is pretty shattering anywhere in the world to be met with such a question.

"Can you read?" I asked him.

No, he was an illiterate herdsman, looking after the family's cattle.

I had in the car a copy of the "wordless book," a small booklet of coloured pages, that we use to help illiterate people to understand the way of salvation. I reached in for it, and then we sat together at the roadside in the early morning sunshine, as slowly and carefully I outlined to this inquirer the way to know the Lord Jesus Christ as his own personal Saviour. Within twenty to twenty-five minutes, I had the joy of seeing him open up his whole heart to receive God's gift of faith, and to believe that Christ had died for his sins, redeeming him from the sentence of condemnation.

I then asked him why he had used that strange phrase: "Are you a sent one from the great God to tell me of the thing called Jesus?"

"Well," he started to explain, "my brother is a teacher."

So often in Africa, all members of a family club together, and out of their scanty means pay for one son to be educated. He will, they trust, become an "earner" and at that time will be expected to refund all he has been lent. This refunding system can be deeply painful and can last a lifetime. The "family" tends to live on the back doorstep of the unfortunate man and demand help on every conceivable occasion. It is not at all an enviable position, and yet education is a coveted blessing. Frequently such a person will seek employment far from his own tribal area, just to escape the harassment of poverty-stricken relatives. Others, bound by centuries of family tradition, stay and eke out a fairly miserable existence and carry the burdens of all. Among those, many are driven to escapism tactics and drown their problems in drink, so I was not surprised to hear the next comment, as my new friend continued his explanation.

"He is not a good man: he is often drunk. He came home from school early the other day, and we asked him why. He told us that there had been a special speaker at school that day.

"'Oh,' I enquired, 'What did he teach?'

"'Well, he told the children that he had been sent to them by a great God to tell them about something called Jesus,' my brother replied.

"'What did he tell them, then?' I queried.

"'Oh, I don't know,' he answered. 'I didn't bother to stay. I went out for a drink.'

"Every day since," my herdsman friend concluded, "when I have been out watching the cattle, I've repeated the phrase: 'A sent one from a great God to tell them about something called Jesus,' and each time I said the word 'Jesus,' it was sweet in my heart. So I began to want to know more."

He prayed, I gathered, though he did not call it praying, "Please, God – if there is a God – would you send me a sent one to tell me of this thing called Jesus?"

We talked for some time, and as we drank a cup of coffee together, I went through the wordless book with him yet again, making him recite after me a Bible verse for each page until he knew these verses by heart. I left him with the booklet, so that he might share the Good News with his family. Taking with me his name and a vague idea of his whereabouts, I eventually drove on. At the next main village, I stopped to look for the African evangelist to tell him of this new convert, so that he might visit his village and talk with his family. Driving on a little further, I remember stopping where the road crosses the river, not this time for a coffee break. I was trembling and needed a moment just to worship God for His abundant mercy and overflowing love. That He had sent me on a 400-mile journey to another country, another tribe, and language group; that He had allowed me to feel sleepy at six o'clock that early morning, in order that I might stop at that clump of bushes, to meet with one man, and he an illiterate herdsman – my heart was filled with a deep sense of awe at the marvel of His grace, so unlike the begrudging, half-hearted concern of man for man.

I recall other occasions, such as when God sent John Mangadima back to his own tribal area; Philip and Nancy Wood from a London surgical practice to a hidden ministry at the Nyankunde hospital; Michael Dramata to form a youth club in his own school hall. The distance involved in the sending was of little importance. What mattered was the willing obedience to go, wherever sent.

John Mangadima and I had worked together at Nebobongo hospital throughout my first and second terms of service. He had only had primary school education when he first joined me. Together we learned what was involved in creating a workable medical service for the large church area, including the establishment of a training school for ward orderlies. Through these years, he had assiduously learned all I could teach him, including a basic working knowledge of physics, chemistry, botany and zoology; a certain ability in rudimentary mathematics; a slightly greater fluency in the French language; as well as a good understanding of anatomy and physiology, surgical techniques and the principles of medicine. Ward rounds and clinics, emergency operations and interventions, we did them all together.

Then the rebellion separated us for eighteen months, and John carried on as best he could. He kept the hospital routine going, maintaining good standards in medicine and in discipline.

When I was enabled to return to the war-torn territory, to help in the enormous programme of rehabilitation, I joined an inter-mission medical team at Nyankunde. There the Evangelical Medical Centre was born, comprising hospital, maternity complex, leprosy, psychiatric, and tuberculosis care units, and an extensive polyclinic for the treatment of some one thousand patients who attended daily. My part was to be the organization of the training school for national paramedical workers – the planning and erection of suitable buildings, the preparation and compilation of realistic study material, the organization and administration necessary to gain government recognition and eventually official diplomas for the graduates. Our aim was to train national medical evangelists who would be authorized and capable of carrying on their ministry in the event of a compulsory foreign withdrawal.

John Mangadima asked to be allowed to join this new school as a student to further his knowledge and to gain government approval for his work, in order that he might better serve the population in his own tribal area. This request set us all thinking and questioning, as there were many others like John, working in our five mission church medical services. The result, three months later, when the new school opened with twenty-four, new first-year students, was the formation of two senior classes. John and thirteen others, already graduated from one of the previous schools as ward orderlies, with varying lengths of practical experience, formed the first of these senior classes. They would do two years of studying to upgrade their diplomas that they might be recognized as government medical auxiliaries. Fourteen others, who had actually been in the older training schools at the outbreak of the rebellion, formed the second group. They would do three years of study to complete their interrupted courses, and gain the new diplomas. The first-year group faced four years of studies for the same recognition.

Subsequently, at the end of two years, John and ten others regraduated, now as auxiliary nurses, the government designation. Their training had been carefully geared to the needs of the population, in order to enable them to act as junior doctors, to diagnose and treat almost ninety per cent of the patients they would meet, and recognizing the need for more skilled help, refer the remaining ten per cent to the centre.

John had done exceptionally well, and all the team at Nyankunde recognized his capabilities and potential for further training. He was invited to stay on at the centre as a member of the staff, to act as assistant director of the college, and also to have special training from one of the surgeons – of the team. He was thrilled at the prospect, involving, as it did, having a brick-built home with electricity and running water, a reasonable government-subsidized salary with the likelihood of annual increments, and an excellent local school up to university entrance standard for his growing family to attend.

It was at that point that I sent for John.

We sat, a little tensely, in my sitting room, looking out over the school dormitories, football field and classrooms, across the valley to the distant mountains. I think he knew what I was about to say.

"John," I began a little fearfully, "you asked to come here to Nyankunde, back to school, to train in order to serve *our* people. But John, they are not here in the mountains ... they are back down there in the steamy forests."

I hesitated. What was I asking of him? Would I be willing to pay the price that I was suggesting that he should pay? "Down there in the steamy forests" 350 miles away, there were over one million people with only the remnants of a rudimentary medical service, carried on by the unstinted love of a band of selfless missionary nurses and a small group of minimally-trained, but very faithful, national ward orderlies. There, a medical leader would not have the fellowship and support of the training team at the centre, with consultations and seminars, with the opportunities for advancement and promotion. His name would not be on the government medical personnel list, nor on their pay sheet. He would have a mud-and-thatch home (which he might well have to build first, as white ants had devastated his old home in his absence). He would inherit the badly damaged buildings of the small forest hospital, which had suffered so much in the rebellion. There was no running water, no electricity. The nearest school for his children's education was seven miles away, with no available daily transport. There was an almost chronic food shortage at Nebobongo. There was no easy way for supplies of medicines and equipment to reach them there.

Slowly, he drew his eyes away from the distant hills and turned and glanced at me briefly. I held his eyes for a moment, before he quickly looked away again. I prayed earnestly that God would make clear to us His way.

At last, he got up abruptly and said he would pray over my remarks with his wife. I watched him leave and make his way down the hillside, back to the hospital. I sighed inwardly. It was a very costly decision that had to be made. How could I ever seek to help them find God's will in this? Dare I accept the responsibility of advising them?

Suddenly another line of thought swept across my mind. Had I really the faith to believe that this move really was of God? Could John ever become the medical director of our church medical services, or was this only a dream, a figment of my active imagination? Had God guided me through the fifteen years of our relationship in preparing John for this specific task?

I asked God very simply to confirm this step as His will, that we might know with an absolute assurance that He was on the throne of our lives, guiding us into the centre of His will and purposes.

On the Friday of that week, I read in the morning from the last chapter of the first book of Chronicles, telling about the death of King David, where the words appear, "and Solomon his son reigned in his stead." My mind raced back to that day, years before, when I started work at Nebobongo, with John as my first student. God had laid on my heart verse nine of chapter two of the book of Exodus:

Take this child, away and nurse him for me and I shall give you your wages.

That day I had accepted from God the responsibility for the newly-born medical service for the WEC church area, and John as representative of the national medical workers in that service. We had "nursed" them. Was this now the culmination of the "wages," to see John as the new medical director (under my authority – in the background – as a medical practitioner)?

John came to me that evening. He said that God *had* spoken to him through the Scriptures, but before he shared this with me he wished to explain a problem that made it hard, both for him and for his wife, to express their guidance.

"You have given us an impossible choice," he explained. I agreed in my heart but said nothing.

"If Nato and I say that we have been called of God to return to Nebobongo," he continued, "everyone will say how marvellous we are, to do without the salary that we would have received had we stayed here. But if we say that we have been *called* to stay here at Nyankunde, no one will believe us. They will just say that we could not resist the pay."

Fairly clear thinking for a forest lad, with very little formal education!

"OK, John, I see that," I agreed readily enough. "As the Lord enables me, let me promise you that I will endeavour to see that you get the same salary, whether at Nebobongo or Nyankunde." We looked at each other, long and searchingly.

"Thank you, doctor," he said very quietly, giving me a long, firm handshake, as he went away to discuss the matter further with his wife and to pray together.

At the end of the following week they came to see me again.

"God tells us to go back to serve at Nebobongo," they shared, almost unemotionally.

John then told me that he had been reading in the second book of Chronicles of how Solomon became king, and how God had told Solomon to ask of Him what he would as he took up his new appointment.

"And Solomon said to God," we read, *"Thou hast dealt with my father David with great loving-kindness, and hast made me king in his place. Now, O LORD God, Thy promise to my father David is fulfilled for Thou hast made me king over a people as numerous as the dust of the earth. Give me now wisdom and knowledge, that I may go out and come in before this people; for who can rule this great people of Thine?"*

"And," said John, "I just know in my heart that that is to be my prayer, as the Lord leads us back home to help our own people."

My heart welled up in praise to God, especially as I realized that the Lord had spoken to John through the same Scriptures that He had used in speaking to me, to confirm that this was of Him. The three of us prayed together, worshipping God for His great goodness, and stating publicly our renewed faith that this was definitely God's will at that time for each of us.

Two months later, with the school two-ton truck loaded with his household goods, furniture and livestock, as well as his wife and family, John was ready to set off on the two-day journey home to Nebobongo. I went down the hill at about 4:30 a.m. to pray with them and wave them off. As I reached up to shake hands with John, he pressed a piece of paper into my hand as we said goodbye to each other. It was a somewhat emotion-filled moment, as John and I had been close friends for fifteen years, and this parting had a certain finality about it that we had never experienced before. I was deeply conscious that I appeared to have the light end of the load, remaining at the comparatively easy job assigned to me at Nyankunde, while they launched into the definitely difficult job assigned to them at Nebobongo.

After they had driven away I slowly made my way back up the hill to my home, recovering my composure and praying for John and his family as they set out on the long, pothole-filled road. Then I unravelled the scrap of paper crushed in my hand and read John's last message to me.

"Thank you, Doctor, for everything" ... and I thought of our years of friendship, fellowship and growth in the service of God and of our community. "Please, you do not need to tell the others, but we do not want the salary."

I reread it slowly, pondering over each word.

My eyes filled again with tears, as I sensed the magnitude of his faith in God. John knew God had called him to the task in our WEC area, centred at Nebobongo, and he was willing to trust God to supply all he would need, not wishing to accept a "shortcut" with my help.

I was deeply touched and challenged. I am not sure that I would have had the faith to take such a stand in a similar situation. John had the faith, to go out to prove the utter faithfulness of God, knowing that He, God, had called them – appointed them – and was thereby committed to provide for them; it was as though he did not want me to interfere in the process!

☼✦☼✦☼✦☼

Philip and Nancy Wood must be free to tell their own story, yet to me they were also great examples of faith launching out in obedience to God's directions. As I have mentioned earlier, Philip was a qualified surgeon, working in a London teaching hospital, with many avenues of advancement open to him. He had an excellent brain and technical ability. As others would have said, he had it "made." There would be no difficulty about promotion or rapid advance up the professional tree.

Nancy was a physician, trained in the Toronto medical school. She too had excellent prospects of getting ahead and doing well. Then they both heard God's directing voice to move out into full-time overseas missionary service. Nancy had already visited us twice at Nyankunde, once on holiday, once as part of her course as a medical student. These visits had sown a seed, showing her the probable field for her future service. As she and Philip prayed and planned, all the bits of the jigsaw began to fall into place, and together they became sure that God wanted them to join the team at Nyankunde.

Four months in Belgium studying tropical medicine and perfecting a fluency in French, four months at mission headquarters taking part in a training programme for missionary candidates, acceptance into the missionary family, farewell valedictory service in Philip's home church, and they were on their way to Zaire within the year!

During our six weeks of overlap, before I finally handed over the direction of the school to them and left on my way home to Britain, I wanted to show them all I could of the medical service for which they would be, in part at least, responsible. So we piled into our valiant two-ton truck and set out on the 350 rough miles to Nebobongo, in the middle of the wet season! Arriving eventually after twenty-eight hours of driving, we had a wonderful week of welcome, mingled with medical refresher courses, daily Bible teaching, fellowship and farewells. The return journey went extremely well. The road was relatively dry and firm, and we travelled easily, at a good steady speed, until 5:30 in the evening. Dusk was just falling.

As we turned a corner and started the descent of a slight hill, we saw a truck, two trucks, three – four – five ... more and more ... parked all along the side of the road. And at the bottom of the hill, amidst a surge of shouting truck drivers, sunk down in a veritable sea of mud, a large twelve-ton truck.

Steep muddy banks flanked the wide stretch of road through the valley, and forest trees and thick undergrowth came almost to the banks on both sides. As far as we could see, over 200 yards of straight road before it curved away to the right in the distance, there was *mud*.

We parked our small van behind the others, piled out, and made our way down the hill to see and hear what was going on.

The situation was almost ludicrous, like an ill-thought-up fairy story. The large truck, stuck deep down in a mud hole, was found to be loaded with over one hundred live and snorting pigs.

During the next hour or so, we witnessed a scene that would have rivalled most pantomimes. The pigs had to be strung together and then unloaded into the mud bath. The truck was then pushed, shoved, heaved and eventually towed across onto solid ground. The pigs then had to be cajoled, beaten, threatened, screamed at and coerced back into captivity, before a totally ungrateful, grumbling "chauffeur" drove off into the night leaving the rest of us to manage as best we could.

Ours was the smallest of the waiting vehicles, so according to an unwritten truckers' law in the jungle, it was our doubtful privilege to go first. We decided that Basuana, our African driver should be responsible for the attempt, but that I should stay with him in the cab to give moral support. The rest of our party, including Philip and Nancy, our house help Benjamin with two of his young sons, and several first-year students for the college, all set out to walk across the valley along the banks flanking the road. Truckers moved ahead of our van in two lines, seeking with their feet some eighteen inches under the surface of the mud for the firmest crests of the ploughed up road. Between those crests, we know only too well, lay deep yawning channels, in some places five or six feet deep.

We followed the men – gingerly, nervously, fearfully, yet steadily. The slightest deviation or slip and we would turn over. The way seemed interminably long, our progress unbelievably slow.

Suddenly we slid!

Despite a valiant effort, shouts on all sides, other drivers rushing to hold us upright, we turned over. The mud slowly and irrevocably sucked us into its waiting chasms.

It was a frightening experience. In the dark, eerily lit by distant headlights, the fear was heightened. Slowly Basuana and I were extricated from the cab, only to sink to waist deep in the foul morass. Dragging one foot painfully up after the other, I stumbled across to the bank, where Nancy and Benjamin, anxiously watching, stooped down and hauled me up to safety.

I was nervously shaken and nearly exhausted. It took very little encouragement from Philip to persuade me to go on, on foot, with Nancy and Benjamin's children to the first village we should find and seek a place to rest, dry out, clean up, and wait. We left Philip, Benjamin and the students at the mud hole with Basuana and the overturned van, and made our way stumblingly forward through the night, up the next hill, to the welcome fireside in the forecourt of a small village.

Shortly after three in the morning, we heard the van and hurried to the roadside. There was Philip, triumphant, and smiling through mud from head to toe! I moved forward and started to apologize to him.

"Whatever are you apologizing for?" Philip queried in surprise.

How could I explain how guilty I felt at having deserted him that night? It was his first encounter with a real mud hole, and maybe my hundredth. I was an old hand at persuading other truckers to help me by using the local language and idioms, whereas Philip had been in the country less than a month and knew practically nothing of the language, let alone how to use it effectively. In such circumstances, I was accustomed to roughing it, working with the rest to shove and pull and dig; Philip had just come to us from a London hospital, a member of a surgical team with hands accustomed to surgeon's gloves, rather than truckers' shovels!

"Come on, cut it out!" he remonstrated laughingly: "This has been the most exciting night of my life!"

And he meant it! I had only been able to see Philip as a London surgeon and so was horrified to see him plunged so early into the rough side of missionary life; but he was so sure, by faith, that he was where God wanted him, that he was as happy to be shoving the van out of a mud hole, as to be operating in a sterile theatre.

So the two of them settled into Nyankunde, to school and hospital life, to take over from me just at the very moment that I needed to be released to go home to help look after my mother. Their quiet assurance of faith in God's direction for their lives has carried them steadily through these intervening years, content in the present-tense achievement of service to those in need in that developing land, and refusing to be troubled by the "might-have-beens" of growing importance and almost certain promotion had they stayed to work in their home lands.

John Mangadima's faith involved guidance to an area two days' truck journey away, in his own home village, among his own tribesmen. Philip and Nancy Wood's faith involved guidance to a land two days' jet-plane flight away, six thousand miles to a different continent.

Michael Dramata, in contrast, had faith to be guided to a needy spot in his own school hall, not one hundred yards from his dormitory! Michael had come to the nurses' training school, as it were, by a back door. He just turned up one evening late in November 1966, two months after school had started. Dusty and tired from a long journey, speaking a northern tribal language and with no workable knowledge of French, he tried to persuade me that he had arrived to take part in our school programme. I tried to assure him that this was impossible. We were almost totally unable to communicate meaningfully and would have inevitably become increasingly frustrated with each other, had Basuana not arrived at that moment to see me about something. He summarily interpreted our meanings to each other, but Michael simply could not take in that I had refused him a place. Had he not walked 200 miles to come? Was he not sure of God's calling and direction? Did I not understand that he had been sent by his church? Wearily I told Basuana to find the lad a bed for the night, see that he was fed, and help him to set out on his return journey the next day.

The following day Basuana came and told me that he had admitted Michael to the school, issued him with a set of uniform clothes and given him a place in the dormitory!

Had my ears deceived me? I nearly exploded. I was school director, not Basuana. What high-handed interference was this?

"Doctor," he remonstrated patiently and quietly, "when you have heard his testimony, you will understand. We just have to accept him. It is clear that God's hand is upon him. He is filled with an amazing assurance of faith and acts on it with one hundred percent conviction. You just cannot refuse him a place when you have heard!"

As often happened, Basuana was right – and Michael was accepted. By interpretation I warned him, however, that his past testimony would not be sufficient to gain him the coveted graduation diploma. He would have to work hard, really extremely hard. During the four-year course of general science and medical studies to become a medical auxiliary, he would also have to cover two years of general secondary education and pass the equivalent government examination to obtain a certificate of the high school "orientation" programme. This certificate was necessary before he could even attempt the final medical examinations.

Michael responded and worked hard. He was a good student and did well, term after term. Besides this, he maintained a consistent Christian testimony, standing fearlessly for what was right and refusing to take part in student activities that were in any way questionable or in defiance of authority.

However, as he started his fourth and final year at the college, I sent for him again and reiterated my warnings.

Without steady, unremitting perseverance at his studies, he would not achieve his goal.

On the first Sunday of the term there must have been an announcement made by the local elder in the morning church service. I am afraid I was not attending sufficiently, possibly using the moment to tick off the students' names in the school register to see that they were all in church as they should be!

On Monday morning Michael met me outside the classroom as I arrived in school.

"Good morning, doctor," he greeted me courteously. Then he added, "What are we going to do about the vandals?"

I looked at him blankly.

"I beg your pardon, but what did you say?" I asked in amazement.

"What are we going to do about the vandals?" he repeated unabashed.

"Michael, I've no idea what you are talking about," I said, "but it is time for school," and I moved past him impatiently. At the end of class there he was, with the same question. Trying to be patient, I asked him to explain himself. "Well," Michael began, the pastor asked us to pray about it in church yesterday."

"Pray about what?" I asked, mystified and almost irritably. "About the vandalism," Michael explained simply and unperturbedly.

It was true that the whole region was suffering from a wave of vandalism at that time. Church windows had been broken, benches in the primary school had been smashed, pineapples and other food in local gardens senselessly slashed to the ground.

"But that is not our affair, Michael," I remonstrated. "That is for the local church to discuss and find a way to help." "Oh," he ejaculated, "aren't we members of the local church here?"

Caught off guard, senior missionary challenged by junior student, I hurriedly assented that we were and made my escape homeward for breakfast.

Next Sunday I listened more carefully when the notices were read out. Imagine my amazed horror when I heard the elder announce a meeting to he held in our own school hall during the coming week!

"Next Tuesday at seven p.m. in the new nurses' school auditorium, there will be a meeting for all vandals under the age of fifteen."

A startled gasp was followed by amused smiles, and not a few heads turned to look at my astonished face. After church I sought out Michael.

"Did you have that notice given out, Michael?"

"Well, yes," he assented, surprised for the moment by my brusque manner. "You had agreed, doctor," he added, placatingly.

On Tuesday evening I went down the hill to unlock the doors and put on the lights, somewhat sceptical as to who might respond to such an unorthodox invitation. Who, in our dignified church congregation, would be willing to identify himself publicly as a "vandal?"

Expecting a handful of curious youngsters who might come for the fun of it, I was utterly unprepared for the sea of urchins that blocked my way to the school. Struggling through them to open the doors, I had no time to get the lights on before they began to surge in. Our hall seats one hundred and twenty. Half that number again mobbed in, sitting three on every two chairs. The noise was deafening; the smell of small, unwashed, sweaty bodies crushed together in a rapidly rising temperature was almost overpowering. They were chewing mangoes. That has to be explained for the inference to be understood ... spitting out the hairy skins and the large stones, sucking out the dripping, succulent flesh, and then wiping their sticky, dirty hands down the nicely whitewashed walls!

"What on earth are we going to do with them, Michael?" I gasped in horrified unbelief.

"I'm going to tell them about Jesus," he replied calmly, quite unruffled by the noise or heat or smell. And that is what he did, week after week. He turned that crowd of undisciplined, noisy, rebel youngsters into a youth club. He taught them Scriptures and songs. He had them in the front of the church on Christmas Day, looking like little cherubs, singing carols and reciting verses!

About the fourth or fifth week there was a good deal of noise outside the hall during the club meeting. Michael asked me to take over the leadership while he went out to see what was going on. I confess that as soon as he left the hall, there was as much noise inside as outside; I simply did not know how to control one hundred and eighty youngsters! At the end of club that evening, when the children had all left and we were tidying up, Michael asked me a shattering question.

"What are we going to do for the senior vandals, doctor?"

"Michael, enough!" I interrupted sharply. "It's quite impossible."

"Doctor," he continued in his usual quiet, amiable way, ignoring my explosion, "when I went outside, there was quite a crowd of young men, eighteen to thirty years old, complaining that it is not fair; we are telling the youngsters about Jesus, but not them."

"Michael, stop!" I cried. "You just cannot squeeze another thing into your timetable and still have any hope of passing your final exams. And I also simply have not the time for one more evening's extra activities."

"Are you really telling me, doctor," he asked patiently, "that you will not tell them about Jesus?"

I fled, defeated.

Next Sunday it was given out in the church notices that there would be yet another meeting in our school hall.

"Next Thursday at seven p.m. in the new nurses' school auditorium, there will be a meeting for all vandals over the age of fifteen."

Amazed incredulity and outright amusement swept through the congregation. I kept my head down in horrified alarm. *Not*, I thought, *that anyone is likely to respond in that age group*. Yet I had learned to dread the consequences when Michael put his hand to something. Things always seemed to happen!

Next Thursday evening every one of the one hundred and twenty seats were filled, with a very motley crew of young men. They represented a complete cross-section of our local community. There were a few church elders, some respected employees from the printing works, and some educated teachers from the secondary school who had all come to assist us, should we need them. Then there were drop-out youths who had been drinking heavily before they came. There were ne'er-do-wells who were chewing and smoking ceaselessly (and in our area, one did not ask what they were smoking). Some had come as much as eight miles from across the valley to see what was going on. From some, I overheard language that was so obscene that I was glad I did not really understand enough Swahili to follow them fully. Whatever would we do with them all?

"Michael," I breathed fearfully, "whatever can we do with them?"

"*You* are going to tell them of Jesus," he reported cheerfully.

So a pattern emerged that we followed every Thursday through that school year. We gave them twenty minutes of current events, covering the blackboard with a huge chalk-drawn map of the world and using the week's news headlines from the radio as our source of information. Then we prepared a twenty-minute, obviously urgently needed lesson on preventive medicine and personal hygiene. We finished with a forty-minute "Bible thriller," largely Old Testament stories told in an up-to-date contemporary setting, so that they might realize how relevant scriptural teaching is for their own everyday lives. In April and May, we had four consecutive lessons on the theology of salvation. On the fifth week, as silence settled on them, I threw out a challenge to them.

"Here is a one Zaire note," I said, holding up a currency note valued at about two dollars. "The first to come for it can have it."

No one moved.

I said it again, waving the note aloft.

Slowly a fellow, halfway back on the left, rose to his feet, looking at me. Heads turned to look at him as they heard his chair scrape on the concrete floor, and many tittered. It was Jackie, a half wit, and all were amused at his credulity in the white lady's offer.

He never took his eyes off me, as he slowly made his way up the side aisle of the hall, getting faster as he approached the front. The last few yards he positively ran toward me, grabbed the note and retreated several feet, looking at me in unbelieving amazement.

"Can I keep it?" he stuttered.

"Of course you can," I said. "Didn't you hear me say, 'The first to come for it can have it'? Yes, it is yours now!" He crumpled the note into a torn pocket, and rushed back to me, grabbing my hand in both his, and pouring out an incoherent torrent of gratitude.

The crowd in the hall were furious! They had been had. They never thought I meant it. And now Jackie of all people had gained the coveted money. There was a suspicion of anger in the rising crescendo of noise. I waited. Quietness fell.

"OK. You can all go home now. That is all I wish to say tonight."

There was a stunned silence. I surely could not mean it? Some had walked miles to be there – just for ten minutes' charade and to be ignominiously sent home?

"That is really all there is to salvation," I explained. "For four weeks I have explained all the Bible teaching to you on repentance and confession, on regeneration and the new birth, on God's grace and the work of the Holy Spirit, and the need for your response by faith. Now it is here for anyone who will receive it. All you have to do is to accept what God has done for you by an act of faith, publicly acknowledge it, and thank God humbly for it … as you have just seen Jackie accept the proffered note and thank me for it. Now I want you all to go home and think about all that you have heard from us this year. If you really mean business with God and want to go on with Him, come back tomorrow, and we will help you individually and personally."

Despite their unwillingness to go and rowdy argumentative dissent to my suggested programme, they eventually scattered. Michael and I then prayed together. We felt the Lord would have us claim eight converts from the crowd, and so we started to prepare for their return the following night. We invited seven other senior students to join us, and together we went through a simple programme for leading an inquirer into a true assurance of salvation. The next evening the nine of us gathered for half an hour of prayer to claim our eight converts. Then we began to realize that there was a growing noise, a quiet sustained murmur, outside the hall. We put the lights on, opened the doors and stood back ... as over eighty young men filed into the hall, orderly and expectant! Among them were a few church elders and print shop employees, who helped us through a most memorable and exciting evening. Right into the early hours of the morning, with pressure lamps and hurricane storm lanterns to light the hall, we had the privilege and joy of helping many of these young men into an assured position of faith in God's salvation.

And all this had come about because a senior teenager had obeyed God. Michael had heard the challenge of God's voice in his heart, to care for the spiritual welfare of these "vandals" despite my warning that in so doing he might seriously jeopardize his chances of passing his final examinations. He apparently ignored me and moved out in faith to obey God's challenge, and God honoured him. Not only were one hundred youngsters formed into a good, disciplined youth club and over eighty youths brought face-to-face with the way of salvation, many coming into an assurance of that salvation for themselves personally but also Michael passed his final examinations with honours!

Then there was Joseph Ndabuyi. He grew up with our orphanage children, many of whom were adopted by us when born to parents suffering from leprosy, often living in our leprosy care village. The children would be allowed to see their parents regularly, though not to be touched by them. Sadly, this gave the youngsters little chance to grow to love their parents. Indeed, some developed a deep revulsion, particularly of those who had severe facial disfigurement as well as resorption of fingers and toes. This was one of the unhappiest aspects of our work in those early days, when leprosy was still a little-understood and fanatically-dreaded disease, and segregation was the only way we could then see of protecting the children.

As a five-year-old, one Sunday afternoon Joseph came to realize that God so loved him individually and by name, that He had sent His only Son Jesus Christ, to die on the cross to pay the price of his sins and to offer him salvation, and in a very real way, the young lad was truly converted.

As an eight-year-old, he rushed into my home one Sunday afternoon after children's church and blurted out breathlessly, "Could I be a missionary, Mummy?"

"Well, but of course Joseph," I answered quickly, a little taken aback, but willing to hear more.

"Teacher talked to us this afternoon about missionaries being God's witnesses, and how God wants us all to be His witnesses. So that means me too, doesn't it?"

"Yes, dear, certainly," I agreed, happily surprised at his responsiveness.

After a moment's pause I asked him if God had given him any indication where He might want him and in what sort of work. Without a word, Joseph burst into tears and rushed from the room. I did nothing, other than pray for the lad and wait for God's timing. About a week later Joseph came in again one evening and stood quietly beside me as I was sewing patches onto boys' shorts. After a while I turned and drew him toward me and waited expectantly.

"Yes," he said, taking up the conversation where we had left off a week before. "Yes, God *has* said where, but I don't want to do it!" There was a break in his voice and a decided tremor in his lower lip.

"What is it, Joseph?" I queried softly.

"To be a doctor like you and work among the people with leprosy," he blurted out, looking up at me with relief that he had told me.

I held his young hands for a long minute and prayed in my heart for wisdom. I could picture so clearly this boy's parents and sense the sadness and revulsion from the smell and disfigurement.

"Joseph," I started off, "that is very wonderful, and one day you will rejoice. At present it is a long way off, a distant vision, and we do not need to look at it too closely now. You hold that in your heart, and thank God for wanting you in His service. Then determine to work hard at school and to learn your lessons well, so that one day it may become a reality. Today you dread it, but when God brings it about you won't dread it then, because God will help you to love the work and the people whom you will serve."

He ran off then to join the other children, and I prayed for God's protecting hand on his young life and for the years that lay ahead. In faith I trusted that God would bring that vision to pass. Much, much was to happen in the intervening years. At times it seemed impossible that the vision would ever be translated into fact. Joseph was not particularly bright at school, but he did eventually pass from our fourth grade primary class to the central senior primary school at Ibambi and went there as a weekly boarder when twelve years old. Then the rebellion came and interrupted his schooling for two years. At last we got him into secondary school in 1966 as a seventeen-year old. He did not pass his entrance exam to the nurses' training school the first time he tried, and we had to wait yet another year. However, he arrived in 1969 and qualified with very good credits in 1973. The way then opened up for him to go to the capital city of Zaire for a special six-months' training course in the care of leprosy patients and their ulcers. In 1974 in his mid-twenties, seventeen years after God had laid on his heart the vision of missionary service "to the patients of leprosy," Joseph was appointed to the care of the leprosy centre at Mabese, the very place where his own parents had been in his childhood.

There are so many others who have known God's clear direction to them to "go and tell" as His witnesses. His ambassadors, charged with the solemn responsibility of the "word of reconciliation." The faith to step out in obedience to the direction of God has come through varying and differing channels, but always it brings peace of heart, a consciousness of being in the centre of His will.

✧✦✧✦✧✦✧

But then there have been others, perhaps less easy to understand. Two highly qualified young nurses, testifying to God's call to full-time missionary work, joined the team at Nyankunde – and within the year, both had returned to their home country, unable to adjust to the apparently primitive conditions still prevailing in our area. The mud dirt in hospital corridors and wards, inevitable in the wet season, carried in on the feet of staff and patients alike, appalled them. Some said that they should never have come to Africa, feeling it was unfair of church boards at home to have accepted them, encouraged them, and sent them out without training and realistically preparing them. Some spoke of the mental trauma to the two girls, returning home with a sense of failure. Others spoke of the large sums of wasted money in the travelling and equipment of the pair.

And yet God, who is able to call and send, prepare and equip, sustain and encourage each one, could He not equally have prevented all this, if truly it were a mistake in His eyes? Could one have the faith to see that even in all that had occurred in this and many similar stories, God was having His perfect way, working all things together for the good of them that love Him? God's economies, like His thoughts, are so different from ours. Maybe there was no waste as He sees it. He had sent me on a 400 mile journey to meet one man, an illiterate herdsman when gasoline was more than ten times the price at home and spare parts for our vehicles almost unobtainable. That just is not the way God counts, when a soul is ready for the reaping!

Maybe these nurses each learned much from the experience of their own inadequacy, of their need of a deeper knowledge of God, or just of the dissatisfaction of serving God to please themselves or to work off a guilt complex from a youthful, unfulfilled vow. Maybe the team had to learn to consider what could be done to improve our standards and decrease the dirt; or what should be proposed for better training and preparation for future candidates; or how we could more realistically welcome newcomers and help them overcome the initial culture shock without undue criticism. If each of us were always open to God's Spirit and His training, no situation would ever be without value.

A keen young missionary arrived on the field, all set to put her very best into service for the Master and the people of the land of her adoption. Within three weeks, she was fatally smitten with an undiagnosed fever. Had something gone wrong? Surely such a death could not be considered glorifying to God, or reasonable in the desperate economic situation of the day? Yet why do we reason like that? Nationals were also struck down. Here they saw that the missionary was no different from them, equally vulnerable to the onslaught of disease, and yet wholly willing to have come to the country, "counting the cost" beforehand. They saw one who was ready and prepared of heart pass into God's eternal presence without a grumble or a complaint, and they marvelled. Was not God doing His work?

Another girl, a nurse, spiritually prepared and well-trained professionally, carefully screened by a selection committee and interviewed by home staff, arrived in a hard land to commence her missionary career with three or four others, likeminded, yet of differing nationalities. Work was heavy, the girls keeping long hours day and night, weekends included, in the clinic. Language was difficult and demanded disciplined study in the heat and dust of that tropical climate. The hearts of the national people were stony and unresponsive to the gospel, despite faithful prayer, preaching, believing and testimony. Nerves became taut; personalities rubbed on each other; trivialities grew out of proportion. There was no one available to counsel and smooth the rough edges of each one involved. Eventually one had to leave the team. A heart was crushed; fellowship was damaged; others felt vindicated when maybe they should have grieved.

Had God made a mistake? Was their faith insufficient for the situation? Or was it all part of an ongoing process, necessary as preparation for each one for the next step of the way? Can we be big enough to trust God to know best in the dark spells as well as when the sun is shining? The cat's eyes in the fogbound road only show up one at a time, but they are still there. God's promises cannot fail. Even when our faith fails to hold on, wavers, loses touch, yet His purposes are unshaken, and the process of their fulfilment continues steadily.

We have seen some workers clearly called to a "closed land," training and preparing in faith, boldly stating their assurance of God's directing grace. They have at last moved out into the land of their calling, triumphant and certain of His perfect timing – only to be rudely thrown out a few months later by a political coup or army takeover or guerrilla offensive. Was God mistaken? Were they wrong in their guidance? Others, after years of patient waiting and quiet sowing in a hard place, have suddenly had their visas withdrawn, because of the irrational behaviour of an outside visitor who, thoughtlessly, broke down all the confidence so patiently built up by the resident. Could God not have kept that visitor out, or at least prevented him from so blatantly transgressing the law of the land and harming Christian testimony? Yet again, short-term enthusiasts have indiscriminately thrown tracts from a car window, quoting as their justification:

Cast your bread on the surface of the waters, for you will find it after many days (Eccles. 11:1).

The Muslim bystanders, seeing these Christians "disrespectfully throwing God's Word on the ground" (as they interpreted their action) have despised them and their Bible, for they themselves would never let their holy book touch the ground; the patient labour of months, or even years, of resident workers has been destroyed by one thoughtless act. How, how was God honoured by this? Why was it allowed to happen?

Over and over again, we come back to His omnipotent sovereignty and perfect predetermined counsel of omniscient will. He cannot and will not make mistakes. Our faith is in Him, not in the outworking that we see among our frail selves in our fallen human nature. Our faith in God is unassailable and unshakeable. He does know the end from the beginning, and He can move me into or out of circumstances in the working out of His total purpose just as He wishes. I am wholly God's, and as I am His servant, He has no need to explain to me the why and the wherefore of His dealings and His methods. God asks of me one step at a time in obedience and in faith. He may only show me one yard ahead at a time; that is enough to establish my faith so that He can equally show me all the other yards ahead in the years to come.

The courage needed to obey, to step out in faith, never changes. In fact, as the years go by, it seems we are often trusted with longer stretches of fogbound road than in the earlier days, when sunshine frequently breaks through with exhilarating encouragement. To return to a place or circumstance of known danger or harassment may require even greater courage than when the danger was unknown and the harassment unexperienced. The courage to return to overwhelming problems that have already crushed; to accept a task already known to be too great and beyond our natural training or experience; to go back in the face of increasing opposition; all these can make it harder and harder to be sure of guidance and the Lord's clear direction. Yet throughout, cat's eyes do appear; and courage is given to take the next step; and faith holds on to believe for further cat's eyes, confirming the first.

Some have continued long years in a straight line of duty, yearning for a word of direction to move out into new fields. Some have nursed and cared for loved ones, doing a routine job at home, with their hearts burdened for some special corner of the overseas missionary field. Silence seems to answer their prayers for guidance, and yet the cat's eyes are there, quietly, consistently, one after another. Then when the basic situation changes, suddenly there is a corner, and the eyes momentarily disappear, only to reappear in a new direction; by faithful obedience, one can move off confidently along the new way.

My guidance took me to Africa, six thousand miles from home.

Others may be led to their next-door neighbour or to a job in their home town with equal certainty and clarity.

The basic fact of God's desire and ability to guide each Christian into his chosen place for their service is in no wise influenced by the geography involved in that guidance. Certainly there is no implication that all Christians must be, or should be, guided into full-time overseas missionary service, even though this was God's plan for me. I have used my testimony simply to illustrate the various ways in which God guides us.

God's guidance includes the circumstances in which we find ourselves, the advice of older Christian friends, examples seen in our daily reading in the Bible, the assurance that develops in our hearts as we pray over a situation, and an increasing consciousness of peace as all these fit together and add up to one solution.

At different times in our lives, one of these means of guidance may be more prominent than another. All have had their part in my own life. Sometimes God does graciously allow us to use fleeces, though it would seem to be the least reliable means of guidance, lending itself to abuse, and possibly stemming from a lack of trust or a desire for haste.

If the parable of following the cat's eyes on the road breaks down, we should not strive to "fit in" or explain away different experiences. A parable is only an analogy and is not meant to be rigidly adhered to in every smallest detail. This parable is meant to encourage and to help us to understand the underlying principle of guidance. This is certainly what the "cat's eyes" have done for me in helping me to comprehend how God would guide me through the problems and decisions of life.

STIR ME TO PRAY

Stir me, oh! stir me, Lord, till prayer is pain,
Till prayer is power, till prayer turns into praise:
Stir me, till heart and will and mind, yea all
Is wholly Thine to use through all the days.
Stir till I learn to pray exceedingly:
Stir till I learn to wait expectantly.

3

STIR ME TO PRAY

Faith in involvement and concern, and therefore in praying

> *"By faith Moses, when he had grown up, refused to be called as the son of Pharaoh's daughter; choosing to rather endure ill-treatment with the people of God, than to enjoy the passing pleasures of sin; considering the reproach of Christ as greater riches than the treasures of Egypt; for he was looking to the reward. By faith he left Egypt, not fearing the wrath of the king: for he endured, as seeing Him who is unseen …*
>
> *"By faith they passed through the Red Sea as though they were passing through dry land; and the Egyptians, when they attempted it, were drowned.*
>
> *"By faith the walls of Jericho fell down after they had been encircled for seven days"* (Heb. 11:24-30).

Why pray?

Does prayer work?

How can my prayer affect a situation?

I do not know the answers, except to state the obvious fact that the Lord Jesus Christ commanded us to pray and set us a vivid example of a life controlled by and dependent on prayer.

I can illustrate my belief in prayer by quoting occasions when prayer offered in one place was simultaneously answered in another, but no one can actually *prove* that

that prayer influenced the situation, or, using the jargon, that "it worked."

Whether my prayer can affect a situation or not may cease to be a relevant question if I can understand the purpose of prayer. If I believe that prayer is the natural outcome of my relationship with God by which I learn to know and understand His will and purpose, and so seek to bring my life into line for its fulfilment, I shall not *primarily* be seeking to "affect situations."

Any understanding of the point or power of prayer demands a real exercise of faith.

Without faith in God, we shall not seek to obey His command to "pray without ceasing." We must believe that God is, that He cares and that He can answer.

Without faith, a living relationship between myself and God, I shall not seek to practise the difficult art of prayer for this is conversation between myself and God, dependent upon that living relationship.

So, if the exchange of the natural spirit of "getting" in my life for the divine spirit of "giving" is evidence of, and the fruit of, faith: if a willingness to be guided by the Spirit of God, and a consciousness of His direction in the comings and goings of my life are the outcome and visible result of faith: so much the more will the practice of prayer only be possible to, and powerful in the life of, a Christian "living by faith." Prayer is the breathing mechanism of faith.

Without faith, I shall not pray.

By faith, I believe in prayer.

God has commanded me to pray. Christ lived in a spirit of prayer and taught us to pray in like manner. As we read the gospel story, we can see just how dependent Christ was on prayer to maintain His relationship with His Father.

In praying, He found courage to vanquish Satan during the temptations in the wilderness. Through prayer, the realization of the authority of God enabled Christ to cure the sick, heal the leper, and cast out demons throughout His ministry (Luke 4:42). Prayer channelled to Him the wisdom of God that enabled Him to reason with the doctors of the law and refute the subtleties of the scribes (Luke 5:16). Through prayer, Christ was guided to choose and appoint the twelve apostles, even knowing that Judas would later betray Him (Luke 6:12). It was through Christ's prayer that Peter was given the great revelation as to who Christ was: *"'Thou art the Christ, the Son of God"* (Matt 16:16 KJV). As a result of His prayer life, our Lord was able to teach His disciples about the suffering of the cross that lay ahead of Him. *"As he was praying"* He was transfigured in glory before the amazed eyes of His three special friends (Luke 9:28). When He descended to the sin-torn world in the valley, it was through prayer that He healed the epileptic boy (Matt. 17:17). In prayer Christ found strength to set His face to go to Jerusalem (Luke 9:51). He taught His disciples through His own prayer life the secret of receiving from the Father all that was needed for their ministry (Luke 11:1-13) .

Christ showed us the courage and fearlessness that we can receive in the face of persecution and opposition. He showed us His deep concern for the salvation of men as He wept over Jerusalem (Luke 13:34) and for all mankind (Luke 22:44). He exhorted us through parables (Luke 18:1, 9) and miracles (Luke 18:38), directly (Luke 21:36 and 22:39-46) and indirectly (Luke 21:37) to *pray* – for ourselves, for each other, for the world.

Yes, prayer is obviously a vital factor in putting God's plan into practice. Not only must I recognize this, I must also believe in the *need* to put God's plan into practice, if I am to take part in prayer effectively.

Do we actually believe that those who have never accepted the Lord Jesus Christ as their personal Saviour are outside the bounds of the love of God, or do we instead try to believe that a God of love will find a way to bring everyone to heaven in the end? Do we reason, "Surely no loving God could condemn to an eternity of suffering people who have never had a chance to hear of the Saviour" without understanding to the full how God's love, His holiness and His foreknowledge all work together to a wholly just judgment? God Himself tells us that He did not send His Son into the world to condemn the world, but to save the world through Him. Men condemn themselves by loving darkness instead of light, by choosing their own way instead of God's grace (John 3:16-21). Of course, if we do think that all men are going to be saved anyway, then prayer is *not* really of any great importance. If on the contrary we believe in Christ's clear teaching that those who do not believe on Him are perishing, then there *would* be an overwhelming reason to pray.

The Bible teaches us that "the wages of sin is death," that is, eternal separation from God, or "being lost." Sin erects a barrier between a sinner and his holy God. That barrier can only be removed by faith in the fact that Christ died in man's place to pay the penalty of sin. Christ Himself bore the curse of sin's condemnation when He died at Calvary.

Christ redeemed us from the curse of the Law, having become a curse for us — for it is written, "Cursed is everyone who hangs on a tree" (Gal. 3:13).

Becoming our sin-bearer, Christ made possible to us an exchange of our sin for His righteousness:

He made Him who knew no sin to be sin on our behalf, that we might become the righteousness of God in Him (2 Cor. 5:21),

this being a free gift to us by His grace:

For the wages of sin is death, but the free gift of God is eternal life in Christ Jesus our Lord (Rom. 6:23).

God's word clearly states that no one else could pay the price of sin. No one else was sinless and therefore able to take our place as our substitute. Anyone else would need to die first for his own sins and so would be unable to die for someone else's sins.

> There was no other good enough to pay the price of sin:
> He only could unlock the gate of heaven and let us in.
> Cecil F. Alexander

If this were not true, if there could be any other way of salvation, then Christ died in vain, and there was no need for Calvary. Would an almighty, omniscient God have given His only begotten Son to die on a cruel cross if He could have found any other way of saving us?

In the light of Calvary, we are forced to admit that all roads do *not* lead to God. Not every religion can provide a way to come to the one and only true God. A religion that denies the deity of Christ and thus His sinlessness, must deny His ability to save us, even by the cross, and so can offer no hope of the forgiveness of sin. Yet without such forgiveness, man cannot approach a holy God. Consequently then, those putting their faith in such another religion must be lost, as they do not know the only way of salvation. Should not this fact too urge us not only to pray for them, that the Holy Spirit might enable them to see the error of their beliefs and lead them to repentance and to faith in the atoning death of the Saviour, but also to go to them that we might tell them of this great provision for their salvation?

Thirdly, believing that prayer is a vital and powerful factor in God's plan, and believing that men do *need* to receive Christ as their Saviour, I also need a *concern* for lost mankind to constrain me to pray. Without that concern, I shall not be willing for the battle that is involved in prayer, as one enters the fight against *"the powers of this dark world and against the spiritual forces of evil in the heavenly realms"* (Eph. 6:12, NIV). Without such deep, heart concern, we shall not be able to continue, to persist and to persevere in this warfare until souls are actually delivered from Satan's power. We shall be defeated and disarmed, by apathy and discouragement, in the first bout of the conflict.

In Hebrews chapter 11 we read of Moses' growing concern for the people of Israel. His concern was such that he chose deliberately – with his eyes open, as we would say – to leave the palace, giving up his right by adoption to Pharaoh's protection and possibly to Pharaoh's succession, and to suffer instead ill-treatment and persecution. He longed to bring about deliverance for his people from the cruel bondage and oppression of the Egyptian tyranny, and in order to do this, he realized that he must be identified publicly as one of them.

Such a rebuttal of influential favour could only bring upon him public disgrace. He knew it. He had counted the cost, but he cared enough for the Israelites to be willing to pay it to the full. He had to flee. He became an outcast shepherd for forty years, and lost all he had grown up to accept as normal. Still, he was sure that this was the right course for him, because "he was looking to the reward." Despite the wrath of the powers of the day, he stuck to his purpose "seeing Him who is invisible."

If we would ask God to give us a like concern for the vast multitudes in the world who are yet without any knowledge of Christ; if we would honestly seek to be identified with the needs of those who are crushed by the cruel despotism of Satan and his evil hosts, held in blindness and ignorance of God's grace and love; if we would allow our hearts to be filled with Christ's compassion for the spiritually blind and hungry, we too would be enabled by God to look ahead to our reward. Christ endured the cross for "the joy set before Him." He could see by faith the fruit of His obedience unto death, that is to say, the salvation of countless millions through the ages, and be satisfied. We too can believe that by accepting God's burden and thereby being driven to pray, we shall see the results in lives set free from Satan's clutches. This will indeed be reward enough for all of us.

To care deeply for lost multitudes throughout the world, and thus to be burdened to pray for their salvation is only possible as we have faith in God and faith in the fact that He is able and willing to answer our prayers. We do not need to know why God is so willing to act in response to our prayers nor how He does it. The reasons and mechanisms are known only to our omniscient and omnipotent God. We know that He has chosen that it should be so. He wants His adopted children to see the needs of others, to be concerned on their behalf, and to show their trust in Him as their Father by bringing that concern to Him in prayer. God has commanded that we should pray at all times – importunate, fervent prayers – believing, persistent prayers.

The harvest is plentiful, but the workers are few. Therefore beseech the Lord of the harvest to send out workers into His harvest (Matt. 9:37-38) is Christ's command to us.

☼✦☼✦☼✦☼

"Till prayer is pain"

Generally in Congo we did not know who was praying for us nor where. We just experienced sudden peace of heart in the midst of fear, deliverance in the midst of danger, healing in the midst of sickness, and we *knew* that God was answering someone's prayer. On a few occasions we learned more details, perhaps to encourage our faith in prayer and to remind us that this is the way that God chooses to act.

The night of October 28-29, in the Congo uprising of 1964 to which detailed reference has been made in other books, is such an occasion. At the height of the awful horror of that night, when I was taken, beaten, brutally humiliated by the guerrilla soldiers, I was briefly tempted to cry out, "My God, my God, why hast Thou forsaken me?" Weeks later we were rescued. Months later, after I had spoken at a meeting near Manchester in northwest England, a lady came up to me.

"I don't want to distress you, doctor," she started hesitantly, "but do you remember the night of October 28-29?"

I certainly did.

"Were you in special need that night?" Most undoubtedly I was.

"I went to bed early that night," she continued, "with a headache. I woke about eleven thirty" – one thirty where I was, as the rebels set about to beat me up – "and your name was in my mind." She did not know me. So far as I know we had never met before, but I was a name on her prayer list. "I got out of bed and down on my knees to pray for you, I went to get back into bed but had no peace, so I woke my husband, and we both got on our knees and prayed for you. Again we went to get into bed but again we had no peace. We stayed on our knees praying for you till one thirty" – three thirty where I was. "We felt the burden lift, and were enabled to return to sleep."

God had met with me in the early hours of that morning. There had been no special vision or blinding light, just a sudden overwhelming consciousness of His presence and power, a great certainty of belonging to Him and of His concern for me and of His ability to undertake for me, no matter what the circumstances. God stirred in me a remembrance of how His Son went to the cross for me with no resistance, and a strange calm pervaded my heart. I began to sense that I was being privileged to share in some little way in the edge of the fellowship of His sufferings. I am not saying that if those two had not prayed for me, God would not have met with me, but I am saying that that is how He chooses to act.

The following day we were again deeply conscious of being upheld by prayer, and by evening we knew something of the story of that prayer. That night at about three thirty, I had been driven away, a captive of the rebels. Eventually word had reached the pastor in our village that "our doctor has been taken captive." He beat the talking drum and called the whole family – men, women and children – to the church to pray for me. It was about four in the morning as they assembled.

In simple faith, certain that a prayer-answering God was concerned and could deliver, they held on, hour after hour, for my deliverance. The church at Ibambi were praying similarly for their white friends, who were also rounded up in the early hours of that morning. At about eleven, an army transport vehicle drove through the village of Nebobongo on its way north to Isiro. Someone ran down to the roadside from the church in time to see twenty or more white foreigners – Catholic priests and nuns, Belgian planters and their wives, our group of Protestant missionaries – at the mercy of a handful of guerrilla soldiers. The rebel guards shouted out that we were being taken to their headquarters in Isiro to be shot.

Back into the church he went with this terrifying news to spur them on to yet more prayer. At first, they told us later, they prayed for our deliverance and that we would be brought back to them alive. Later as the hours passed, they felt led to pray more that we would be kept in peace whatever came to us, and that if we were to die, it would be a triumphant death "singing the praises of our Saviour."

At 2 p.m., we stood to attention in three groups in front of the territorial headquarters of the rebel troops, as the bugle blast announced the arrival of the colonel. We were prepared to be shot – and we were singing praise to our Lord and Saviour, our hearts filled with peace and even with joyful expectation!

After a few moments of wild, strange argument between different factions of the rebel army, we were ordered back into the truck. After several delays and uncertainties, we eventually started the long, stiflingly hot return journey, lurching into Nebobongo, tired and dirty, at 5 p.m. The family were still in church! They had thought nothing of weariness or hunger. For thirteen steady hours they had held on, persevering in believing prayer for our deliverance – and God had brought us back to them! It was a tremendous and emotional welcome home.

"Till prayer is pain" – yes, we saw something of it that day.

Three days later on 2 November 1964, I saw another strange answer to "painful" prayer. After the declaration of independence in 1960 a very sad situation came about in the church in Zaire. Whites and blacks, foreigners and nationals, missionaries and church elders, who had lived closely together in Christian friendship and trust through the years of development of the local church, were suddenly divided from one another by a barrier of distrust. For years, the nationals had accepted unquestioningly the foreigners' use of any available money, almost all of which came from overseas sources. The nationals never doubted the missionaries' absolute integrity, nor even their right to decide how the funds should be used. Now, suddenly, other nationals in neighbouring areas were being placed in positions of authority and leadership (including the handling of the finances), as foreign businessmen and plantation owners were evacuated with their families, because of the threatened breakdown of law and order. In the main, the missionaries did not leave and so retained their leadership and administrative posts. This caused nationals to question our motives and our integrity. Why had we not handed over, as others had done? Why did we not trust them with the money and disbursement of funds as others were being forced to do? We had trained them for leadership – or we had said we were so doing – during all those formative years, so why were we now unwilling to take our hands off? Did we not trust them? Had we something to hide?

The battle became entrenched and threatened to become bitter. I struggled long and hard in prayer over the issue (as I know many others did). I spent hours alone with God, pleading for a solution, for a baptism of unity among us all, a renewal of trust. There seemed to be no answer, but rather an ever growing disunity and lack of trust. Some things were said at church meetings that grieved our hearts deeply, things that should never even have been thought, let alone voiced publicly. The situation was becoming intolerable, when, overnight, we were plunged into the greater bitterness of civil war, the "Simba uprising" of 1964.

The foreign missionaries were caught in the middle of this war as innocent pawns who later became useful hostages. After some ten weeks of alternate threats and reassurances, there came the night when I was first taken captive by the guerrilla soldiers, a night during which I was beaten up and badly bruised. The following day, many of us were rounded up and taken off to the local township to be shot. Reprieved, we were brought back through Nebobongo to Ibambi, where we were put under house arrest. A few days later, we were again rounded up and led out onto the veranda of the house where we were held prisoners, possibly to face a firing squad yet again. Bruised and battered as I was from the previous beating, I stood leaning on a stick, my face swollen and a jagged gash below my right eye. The sergeant, apparently in charge of the present crowd of rebels, shouted at me to know the cause of my sorry state.

"One of your fellows beat me up last Friday," I retorted.

"Liar," he shouted at me, and I shrank back against the wall, as I thought he would strike me in his anger. I did not then know that the rebels were under orders not to touch the white women.

"It's the truth," I defended myself. "I can name him for you."

"All right!" he retorted, "we'll hold a people's court."

After some further interruptions, and various changes of direction in the thinking of the rebel soldiers, including taking away the young American missionary, Bill McChesney, we were bundled unceremoniously back into the house. We did not see Bill again before he and Jim Roger, a Scot, went to be with the Lord through the wicked cruelty of the rebel assassins.

The next day I was collected and taken to a "people's court." The rebels had rounded up all the local men they could find, including, I remember, Pastor Ndugu and some of our evangelists. Some of their wives and children stood around fearfully, and menacing armed soldiers circled the crowd. They had been, and were being, intimidated into agreeing with the purpose and mechanism of a people's court, and told that at a given signal they would all announce loudly and clearly that I was a liar. When asked what punishment was suitable for my crime, they were to shout the dreaded word: *"Mateka! Mateka!"* Literally, it would seem to mean: "Destroy her, destroy her."

The proceedings started. The sergeant asked me endless questions about exactly what had happened at Nebobongo the previous week. Even at that time, within one week of the events, it was hard to remember exactly and precisely, and it was all too easy to be tripped into an apparent inconsistency. As well as this fear, I did not wish to rehearse in public the horrors and humiliation of that night. I dropped my voice. The sergeant struck me across my already-bruised face with the flat of his hand. I recoiled in pain – and spoke up. The moment came for public denouncement. I was taut with fear, knowing I must die, but not knowing how.

Suddenly a strange sound reached my ears and the ears of my legal tormentor. He looked up, astonished. I had never heard the sound before and surely never shall again. Strong men broke down and wept.

All that could be heard rasping against an eerie background of strange silence was the sobbing of hundreds of Africans.

In that moment, they had suddenly seen me as *their* doctor, the one who had loved and served them for twelve years, doing their operations, caring for them in suffering, sometimes bringing their wives' babies into the world in difficult cases. And they were ashamed – bitterly, heartbrokenly ashamed – that one of *them*, an African, had beaten me up and humiliated me. (It did not particularly matter that I happened to be the person concerned; it would have been the same reaction, whichever of the missionary family had been taken captive.) They could not bear the sense and burden of guilt by association – black men identified with one black man. They wept.

In that moment, my heart overflowed with a rush of deep love for these people, our family, my fathers and brothers, who had become so close to me through those twelve years of tremendous and happy service. We were one; nothing could divide us.

It was almost as though we all looked up at the same moment, and a great light shone among us. God had answered, for me, four years of earnest, believing prayer. He wrought unity. He broke through all the distrust and suspicion and brought us into a heart unity that never again was to be broken, however much it might be tried. As I had prayed and prayed in faith, believing for this restored black/white unity, I had had no idea how God might bring it to pass or to what extent He might ask me to become personally involved in the answering of my own prayer.

By awesome deeds Thou dost answer us in righteousness, O God of our salvation (Ps. 65:5).

Brother Andrew in chapter ten of his book *Battle for Africa*, subtitled *What Can You Do?* speaks of our need to identify with the people for whom we pray. I would love to quote the whole chapter (or even better, I would encourage my readers to digest the whole book), but the following will illustrate my point.

"What can I do? you ask. "How can I personally make a difference:" You can help the cause of God ... by being willing to care, willing to learn, willing to suffer, willing to give, and willing to go.

The section on "willing to suffer" includes the following:

I feel very strongly about the responsibility of Christians in freedom to minister to those in bondage.... Half the world's population is behind barbed wire today, living in countries where their worship is challenged and their freedom restricted. It is obscene for those of us in free countries to be so absorbed in ourselves that we forget our suffering brothers and sisters ... We must be willing to minister to them by suffering with them. It is not enough just to pray for the suffering church in a perfunctory manner, as if it were merely one more item on a long laundry list of prayer requests. The Bible teaches that we can actually pray for our suffering brethren in such a way that we vicariously suffer with them! ... To pray effective intercessory prayers, it is not enough to pray once-over-lightly, without focusing on what one is doing. Sit still; block out other distracting thoughts; wait until you can actually visualize that person in a jail cell – or wherever – then pray for him as if he were your own son or father. God will answer that kind of prayer.

Do we catch the spirit? Are we convicted and troubled by it?

We hear that almost every pastor in a certain country overrun by Communism is either dead, or jailed, or in a centre for brainwashing and indoctrination. How can I enter in to pray for them? Let me pause for a moment and imagine one such pastor standing in a small cell with three other men, jailed for murder. There is no room to sit down, let alone lie down. They have been standing twenty-four ... forty-eight ... seventy-two hours; my knees begin to feel weak and my head dizzy. There is no sanitation, and the stench in that tropical land is appalling; my stomach begins to heave. The three companions keep up a running commentary of blasphemous filth ... "Oh, God!" I cry out, "keep that poor man sane! Bring some verse of Scripture to his tortured mind. Block his ears, God, to all the filth. Give him superhuman strength to stand it!" – yes, now I am beginning to pray, as I enter in, in some little way, to the pain of his sufferings.

"Till prayer is power ..."

Sometimes we saw most dramatic and wonderful answers to prayer for the healing of different patients in the hospital. In my second month in Congo in 1953, I worked for four weeks at the government Red Cross hospital at Pawa, to gain the required official recognition of my degree to allow me to do medical work in the Belgian colony. Early one morning on the ward round we saw in a dirty side room, empty of all but the bare necessities, an eight-year-old schoolboy dying of tetanus. He was in the last stages of the disease with almost continuous convulsions, despite an intravenous drip containing sedatives and pain-killing drugs as well as the specific antitoxin. With a cursory word to the careworn parents crouching against the grimy wall, watching in pitiful agony each twisting convulsion, the Red Cross doctor had left the room and continued to the next. Almost casually he had remarked to me that the boy came from our church school at Ibambi.

Later in the day after six hours of surgery, wearily preparing to cycle the fifteen miles home to Nebobongo for the night, I remembered the lad and felt an urge to go back and see him. I wondered how I could communicate with his parents, as I had as yet practically no working knowledge of Swahili. I stood and looked at the emaciated, taut little form and felt a strange mixture of revulsion and pity. I turned to the parents. They had not moved, only their eyes were fixed on me with an unnerving despair.

"Do you love Jesus?" I blurted out, with my limited vocabulary.

They made no sign of understanding me.

"I do," I continued nervously. "I will pray for your son." I turned to the boy and gently placed my hands on his burning forehead. I prayed in English, earnestly and urgently. As I prayed, I sensed a flood of believing faith well up in me. I claimed his complete healing, and I actually felt the fever leave his body. My own body became burning hot. I began to sweat and shiver. I believe the fever passed from him to me. A rush of love for the boy poured through me, as I continued to pray for him. Then as quickly as the pressure had come upon me to pray for him it left me, and I was limp and exhausted. The boy lay still, eyes closed. A slight tremor seemed to shake him and he slowly opened his eyes and looked at us, as if from a great distance. He turned over restlessly and then fell into a deep sleep.

I left then and cycled home, dead tired and aching all over with a high temperature. Next day the two senior missionaries with whom I was staying drove me to the hospital, in order that they might talk and pray with the boy's parents. He was better. He had no further convulsions. His temperature never went up again at that time. God had graciously spared his life and healed his body.

The following year, there was young Nedbiada, a four or five-year-old. Jessie Scholes, one of our senior missionaries, had taken me to a women's meeting one Thursday afternoon. Nedbiada was there with her mother. Jessie spotted her first and went over to talk to her mother. She brought the two of them to me. I examined the child, who had a large ungainly swelling in the upper jaw, disfiguring the whole left side of her face. Her nose was pushed over to the right, her left eye almost closed, her mouth open as the swelling pressed downwards, pushing teeth and gums outwards. In herself, the child was well. There seemed to be no pain, and as yet only minimal signs of malnutrition from an inability to eat. It seemed, as near as I could ascertain, that the growth had first become noticeable some four or five months earlier.

I was fairly certain that it was a Burkitt's tumour, a cancerous growth that appeared to be fairly common in our area among this age-group. There was nothing I could do for the child. In those early days we had not yet the anticarcinogenic drugs that are available today. The thought of attempting any sort of surgery to alleviate the immediate disfigurement and discomfort was appalling to my non-surgical mind.

Under considerable pressure to do all I could, we took the mother and child home with us to Ibambi. The church elders prayed for her. Reluctantly and fearfully I agreed to do what I could surgically on the following Thursday. On Wednesday I was taken ill with an acute attack of malarial fever. On Thursday when I should have been operating, I was lying tossing and turning on my bed with a raging fever. Naganimi, my close friend and helper, talked with Jessie Scholes, and together they took Nedbiada to the Bible school. Here students gathered with local church elders, and together they laid hands on Nedbiada, anointing her with oil and praying for total healing. As they prayed, "it came away," to quote Naganimi!

She gathered up, in a kidney dish, the foul mass as it separated from the jaw. We later sent this to England in formalin, for confirmatory diagnosis that it was in fact a Burkitt's tumour. The bony swelling remained; the unsightly disarray of features was at first unaltered. Slowly over the ensuing months, the gums withdrew and second teeth appeared. As she grew up, the swelling subsided, the eye and nose became rightly orientated, and today, with children of her own, it would be hard to find any remaining external sign of the cancerous growth of her childhood. God had healed.

Several years later, one day during a ward round in the men's medical ward, I was arrested by a sharp feeling of restraint as I approached bed number five. Confused and uncertain, I moved on to bed six and completed the round. As we were leaving the ward, the man in bed five called a male orderly over and asked why the doctor had not examined him. Troubled in my spirit, I sent a message to him, asking him to wait. Then I sent a nurse to call the hospital evangelist. I explained to Agoya the strange certainty in my heart that God Himself had prevented me examining and treating that particular patient. I did not know the man. He was a new patient, his sickness as yet undiagnosed. As Agoya and I prayed together about him in my office, together we became convinced, that God was telling us that He Himself would heal this man.

We returned to the ward. Agoya was amazed when he saw the man, but he did not tell me till later who he was. I examined him and found him to be in an advanced stage of miliary tuberculosis, quite certainly unable to live for more than a few days. Trembling, I wrote the diagnosis on his treatment sheet and raised my eyes to Agoya's. Then we explained that God had told us that He would heal him. We anointed the patient with oil and prayed for him in the name of the Lord Jesus – but in a sense this was only an act of obedience, as I believe the healing had already commenced. Within two weeks the man left us, walking upright, breathing normally, without cough or sputum, and with no remaining sign of the devastating terminal illness that we had witnessed a fortnight before. God had healed him. Yet this man, an evil witchcraft doctor of the local chieftain, possibly also involved in cannibalism, never repented of his sins and never sought God's pardoning grace. I was stunned. Why did God heal him, for whom we had only been led to pray on the one occasion, and yet He did not always heal others for whom we prayed constantly and perseveringly?

There was a wonderful occasion during the frightening months of the rebellion, early in 1965, when a healthy baby was born in answer to believing prayer. Medically this had been impossible. The little crippled mother, limping badly from a combination of childhood rickets and youthful poliomyelitis, had a pelvis through which, by no stretch of imagination, could a normal baby ever be born. In 1962 I had performed a Caesarean section for this woman when she had a living child. We had then warned her that she must always return to us when expecting a child, as she would need surgery every time.

During the rebellion Damaris Banakiamonu, our senior midwife, had gone into hiding in the forest with some of the babies from our orphanage, protecting them from the threatened cruelty of the guerrillas. One day a teenage girl was sent to search for Damaris to urge her to go to the help of a woman, in a forest clearing some miles away, who was having difficulty in giving birth to her second child. Leaving the teenager to care for the orphaned children and following the scanty directions she had been given, Damaris set off to give what help she could.

As she came into a clearing and saw the woman lying on the ground by a hurriedly-made leaf hut, her heart nearly failed her. "I knew her at once," she said, as she recounted the incident to me a year later. "Two years earlier, doctor, you had done a Caesarean section for her, to give her a live baby and you had told her she could never have a normal birth; any time she became pregnant, she must come back to the maternity unit for us to operate on her." She paused, reliving the awfulness of that moment.

"What could I do? Nothing. I would have to sit and watch her and her unborn baby die. I could do nothing at all." Damaris told me how she sat there, holding the woman's hand and searching for words to speak comfort to her, and if possible, to bring her to a saving knowledge of Christ – but her own heart was so full of grief and the frustration of knowing what should be done and being unable to do it, that she could hardly keep her tears back.

"As I sat there praying," she continued, "a voice seemed to say to me, 'Damaris, can you believe?' – and I slowly answered, 'Lord, you know I believe.' I was enabled to put my grief to one side and to start talking to the woman, and those squatting around watching, about the love of God and of His Son, Jesus Christ.

"Suddenly again, insistently, the voice broke through into my heart," she went on, her voice thrilling as she remembered so vividly the whole incident. "'Damaris, do you believe?' – and I answered Him, 'Lord, is it for this woman's salvation you're asking me to believe? If so, yes indeed I can and do believe,'" and I began to tell her more earnestly and more joyously of Christ's death for her on the cross and His gift to her of eternal life if she would but believe and accept Him.

"Again, with a strange, new persistence, 'Damaris, will you believe *now?*' – and startled, I realized that He, the Lord God, was asking me to believe that He could give this woman a living child! Instinctively I felt sure He couldn't, yet immediately I knew that was all wrong – of course He could – He was and is Almighty God but ... my heart seemed to miss a beat at the enormity of what

He was saying to me – *me*, a jungle forest woman – with nothing, no real education, no ability, just nothing, a nobody. My thoughts were in turmoil – yet I sensed that He was waiting for my answer. I whispered back to Him out of my fears and dismay a frightened, 'Yes, Lord,' and felt a longing to add, 'Help Thou my unbelief.'

"Immediately, the voice spoke clearly in my heart, 'All right – tell them'."

She paused again, for a long drawn-out minute, resavouring all her reactions. It had been one thing to tell the Lord in the secret of her heart that she believed He could do this impossible thing, but to tell these scared and waiting women was another thing altogether. What if she had been mistaken in what she thought God was saying to her.

Taking a deep breath and fighting down a mixed sense of fear and awe, she told the little group that God had spoken to her and said that He would give this mother a living baby.

Immediately after she had spoken, she felt faith well up in her heart, and she just knew it was true. She sent one woman off to get water, another to get a fire going, others to collect the leaves they use as cloths. These latter they sterilized in the fire and stripped them of their central vein, working them till they were soft and supple. They did all they reasonably could to ease and comfort the mother as her labour continued, Damaris watching in quiet, exultant wonder.

And God gave her a lovely baby boy.

There was a long silence as she finished her story – and my heart filled with wonder at the stark reality of naked faith in this simple, devout woman, and with awe at the greatness of Almighty God who had stooped to fulfil her faith in an act of mercy and love, a stupendous act of the humanly impossible, a simple act of our miracle-working, eternal God.

Three years later, in 1969, another surgeon of our Nyankunde Medical Centre was visiting Nebobongo on the routine monthly tour of the Flying Doctor Service. This crippled woman came to him, expecting her third baby. After careful obstetrical examination, he decided that he must operate and deliver her child by Caesarean section. Damaris told him all of the above episode. Stirred, he re-examined the woman, but felt he must go ahead in the face of the clear physical indications of her need of surgery – and he found her bony pelvis as I had found it seven years previously, totally unable to allow a normal delivery. God in His infinite wisdom had not re-moulded her bones – no, He had given her a baby by miraculous intervention at the time of her need and in answer to the unquestioning faith of His servant Damaris. To Him be all the glory!

When I look back over twenty years in hospital service and recollect and bring together a few such miraculous stories of healing, stripped of all the surrounding turmoil and activity, the daily medical practice and surgical interventions, the countless other situations in the jostle and noise and sweltering heat of our ordinary lives, with outpatients and wards and clinics, it all sounds so easy and matter-of-fact. It could lead us to assume that these few stories I have given were meant to set the pattern for all the rest, but this does not appear to be the case. The love and concern and prayer were the same for countless other patients where we did not see any dramatic humanly-identifiable healing.

We prayed for all who came to us for medical help, perhaps particularly for those hospitalized. We talked with each one of them about our great God, our faith in Him, and telling them of His power to heal those who trusted in Him. If any asked us to anoint them with oil and specifically pray for their healing in the name of our Lord Jesus, we always agreed happily and the church elders would gather around them for this simple act of believing faith in obedience to God's command to us in the Bible.

Is anyone among you sick? Let him call for the elders of the church, and let them pray over him, anointing him with oil in the name of the Lord (James 5:14).

Equally every patient, many hundreds of them year after year, would be examined, their diseases diagnosed, and treatment commenced to the best of our ability. Some sixty or more each year, in the early days, would undergo major surgery. The majority recovered in the normal course of hospital practice. A few died. Some were apparently healed, whom we had expected to die. Some died, despite hours of believing prayer. We did not ask why but accepted that our God is sovereign. Our task was to obey and to serve to the limit of our God-given ability, trusting Him with the outcome.

The prayer that was offered on our behalf during the five months of rebel captivity in 1964 can never be measured nor its effectiveness estimated. We only know that God heard and answered. Each one of us, nationals and foreigners, can tell of amazing situations when we were just so conscious of the power of prayer. There was a Sunday early in the uprising which would be a case in point. A Greek lady from a nearby plantation had given birth that night in my home to her firstborn baby. She and I were resting on the Sunday afternoon following our busy night of activity, when there was a sudden shattering hammering at the back door. The by-then familiar shout of the rebel army demanded that I "open up in the name of the Army of Liberation."

I stumbled to the door and somehow forced myself outside, pulling the door shut behind me, in an attempt to prevent the soldiers entering the house and thereby further disturbing the anxious mother and her newborn babe. I faced three soldiers, the central one obviously their leader, the man to my right carrying a spear, and the one on my left with a gun slung over his shoulder and a rubber truncheon at his waist. They started demanding money from me. I could not as yet understand much of their language, though I picked it up quickly enough in the weeks that lay ahead, but I could understand the gesticulations and menacing behaviour. However, I did not intend to part with money or any of our property to these evil men unless I was absolutely forced to, so I began to parley and reason with them.

They could not really understand my language, but they soon realized that they were not getting what they wanted. Tempers flared quickly and dangerously. The leader turned to the man on my right and ordered him to strike me down. He raised his spear to drive it through me. He was not a yard from me. Something in me froze. I cannot now honestly say what one thinks or how one reacts in such a situation. Self-preservation is a very strong, instinctive force. I probably raised an arm to parry the blow. Would I live or die? Could I survive the next ten seconds? Was this the end?

"Please, God, if I'm to die, may it be by the first blow!" an agonized gasp heavenward escaped my numb brain, feeling certain that I could not face mutilation. Someone somewhere was praying for me.

After an unbelievably long ten seconds of paralyzed time, I slowly turned my head. The man stood there, his arm upraised, spear poised to strike, eyes filled with anger, yet unable to move. I gazed at him, almost unable to take in the fact that he was "fixed," immobile, arms and legs held as in a vice by a power that he could neither resist nor overcome.

"Strike her down!" roared the leader to the second man.

He raised his gun to crash the butt end down on my skull. Again acting under the impulse of instinct, I raised an arm, bracing myself for the blow, prepared to live or die, turning my head away, holding my breath, my mouth parched and dry. Everything seemed to be arrested in one long, tortured pause....

Again nothing happened.

Slowly I turned. The taut coil inside me began to unwind. The second soldier stood there, as the first, held in the iron grip of an unseen force, totally incapable of deliberate movement at the instigation of his own will. Hatred, anger and fear moved across his face. My eyes held his for a long moment of time, and I let out my breath.

Turning to the leader, I was suddenly conscious of an overwhelming sense of peace, security and power. Prayer around the world on our behalf had released this almighty outpouring of omnipotence. I was saved.

"You're wasting time," I commented dryly. "My God in me is stronger than yours in you. You'd better go around to the front of the house, and we'll discuss this calmly there."

I backed into the house, shutting the door between us before my knees gave way and I crumpled to the concrete floor. I was nervously exhausted, yet filled with a deep sense of thanksgiving to God who had chosen to move so signally on my behalf. I called my house lad and together we prepared and served coffee to the three guerrilla soldiers.

As soon as the back door had closed between us the two men were released from the power that bound them, deeply afraid before this unknown God who had overpowered them so dramatically. Over coffee on the front veranda, Aunzo and I talked to the three about the Lord Jesus Christ. I told them the story of Daniel and the lions' den and how Almighty God had closed the mouths of the ravenous beasts so that they should not touch or harm His faithful servant. I explained how God had acted for me in a remarkably similar way as they, the "lions" (as they were called in the local language), had sought to kill me. Even as I spoke with them, my heart was filled with a great sense of humble awe that the Almighty should care for me in such a way; I *knew* that prayer was being offered for us in faith, believing in God's power to deliver us.

Shortly afterward, called out one evening by a couple of guerrillas because their vehicle had broken down, I found myself walking along the dark road alone with these evil men, surrounded only by the eerie stillness of the forest and the screeching of the cicadas. Having looked at their car and realizing that we probably could mend it for them, I returned with one of the rebels to our village for help.

Along the road this youth said to me almost jocularly, "Aren't you afraid to be walking alone with a 'lion'?"

Little did he know the depth of fear in my heart. I was having to force my mind to think, my legs to walk, and my heart to pray: fear was almost paralyzing me. "Oh, no," I replied, with outward calm and a sudden conscious awareness of inner peace, even in the midst of the fear. "There is a much stronger Lion walking on the other side of me!"

Shocked, he leaned across me, peering into the dark to identify to whom I was alluding. Seeing no one, feeling puzzled or angry, he demanded to know what I meant.

"Our Lord Jesus Christ called Himself the Lion of Judah, and He walks with me always," I answered him steadily, though inwardly trembling.

The stripling, for this brazen soldier was barely seventeen years old, suddenly and unexpectedly broke into tears.

Completely taken aback, I urged him to sit down on the bank at the side of the road. Through sobs, he brokenly told me of his Christian parents, his father a Methodist pastor, who had prayed for him all his life; of how he had rebelled and run away from home and school and joined the new, exciting guerrilla band; of how he had been drafted north a few months ago; of some of the atrocities he had seen and been ordered to take part in; of deep sickness of heart and revulsion of mind against the whole terrible system.

It all poured out into the still darkness of the night, just a lost boy longing to go home. I pointed him to the cross and God's unfailing mercy, grace and love, reminding him of the parable our Lord had told us of the prodigal son and his return to the loving, waiting father. We prayed together and knew His peace in our hearts.

And I *knew* with a great certainty that Christians were praying for me just then. Whoever they were, wherever they were, they could not possibly have known what was my need at that precise moment, but God had known the need and how to meet it. Someone had prayed, prompted by the Holy Spirit, believing that God would undertake for me just then, whatever my need might be. Their obedience to this urge of the Spirit, as they were made to think about me and pray for me, was the link that God wanted that He might act on my behalf.

✿✦✿✦✿✦✿

"Till prayer turns into praise…"

How many more illustrations should I give to prove that prayer works? Answers to prayer can so frequently stir us to praise. This is not always easy; in fact it may be very costly. Spiritual praise that is pleasing to God may have to be sacrificial.

> *Let us continually offer up a sacrifice of praise to God* (Heb. 13:15).

> *He who offers a sacrifice of thanksgiving honours Me* (Ps. 50:23).

When we first found that we were caught in the civil uprising in August 1964 a truckload of soldiers had driven into our hospital compound, carrying with them "a wounded civilian who had been shot in the chest," as I was duly informed by the rough, uncouth leader of the group. That phrase had slowly bitten deep into my mind, setting the stage for the coming months of suffering. "A civilian" must mean that we were at war. What war? Who was involved? Did the outside world know? "Shot in the chest" was to be our first war wound. What would follow? With my grossly inadequate experience and our grossly inadequate supplies, how could we cope with such emergencies?

This particular wound was minimal. The bullet had struck the man over his breastbone, had been diverted along his collarbone and had come out over his left shoulder. There were two neat holes – not even a trace of blood. We cleansed the wound thoroughly, put on two small sterile dressings, gave him two aspirins and a cup of coffee, and admitted him to a hospital bed, as we were obviously expected to do. Three days later he left us, healed and well, and thinking we were rather wonderful! We in turn knew that God had been very gracious to us and we gave Him all the glory.

Fifteen weeks later, on the 26th of November, two days after the dramatic deliverance of nearly two thousand white prisoners from the beleaguered city of Kisangani by the Belgian parachutists, all the whites in our area were rounded up and taken into closer custody at the rebel headquarters. We had a long day of exhausting, petty harassments and growing fears as to what would happen next. Seven of us, missionaries from Ibambi, two men and five women, were eventually hounded into a room in a small three-roomed house and held there by armed soldiers.

Somewhere around ten at night, the leader of our group of guerrillas came into the room and called me out alone. These were moments we dreaded. While we remained together, we could maintain at least some mob courage, but when one was singled out, we knew instinctively that it was for evil. I stood nervously at the leader's table, where he was doing some paper work. After a short time he came over to me and ushered me out onto the steps at the front of the house. It was a dark night, but in the courtyard there was a huge bonfire and a crowd of wild youths dancing round it, under the influence of drink, drugs and witchcraft. They were singing lewd songs, shouting obscenities, and every so often, screaming out to the authorities to throw the five white women to them, declaring, "We know what to do with them!"

With that as a frightening background, the rebel leader came close to me and, attempting to put an arm round me, began to make love to me. I shrank back. As a woman, every instinct in me compelled me to thrust this man away from me. He should not touch me or come near me. But yet I was afraid. If I pushed him off he might strike me, and I had already been so beaten up that I felt I could not stand another blow. Struggling in a vice of intensely conflicting emotions, my mind was caught unaware by the horror of his next words.

"If you will agree to become my wife, I promise you that the four other women will not be touched."

Slowly the words registered in my stunned mind, but I could not think. Apparently I was being offered an alternative; I was being asked to make a choice. Yet there was no alternative, no possible choice. The stark reality worked its way to the surface of my mind. The "four other women" were my field leader's wife in her mid-sixties and three single ladies like myself. Their safety was being promised. My intelligence told me that that promise was utterly worthless, wholly unreliable, yet my emotions tried to grasp and put content into what was being said.

Then the alternative loomed up in horrifying clarity. I would be taken away to a forest village, hidden ... Our rescuers would come, but no one would know where I was, and I would be left behind!

The guerrilla leader took my silence for acquiescence, I suspect. He led me back into his room and gave me a stool to sit on by his table. After a short time he sent for a soldier and told him to escort the other six missionaries across the compound to another house and to see they had everything they needed. Then he was to come out, lock the door, and stand on the veranda to see that they were safe and undisturbed for the night. I had to sit there and watch my colleagues file past me in silence, leaving me alone.

The minutes dragged past like hours.

It was probably only ten minutes, but it seemed like a lifetime, when a great commotion was heard out in the courtyard. A truck drove in; men shouted; a shot was fired; noise filled the night air. The leader went out to see what was going on, leaving me alone. The noise continued. At last, he came back into the room, accompanied by a sergeant major of the rebel army in full uniform. They were talking together rapidly in their language which, by then, I could largely understand. The sergeant major explained how the planes had come that morning, like white birds, over Isiro, fifty miles to the north. The Belgian troops had parachuted onto the runway, and after a sharp, intense battle, the invaders had taken the airport and rushed the town. Severe street fighting had broken out; many were killed. Greek tradesmen still at liberty had grabbed guns and fought with the "invaders" against the guerrilla forces. The latter withdrew to regroup, and in a rapid manoeuvre, all but one of the two hundred white prisoners were rescued, rushed to the airport and flown out to safety.

Even in my stupor of fear, my heart was still able to respond with a sigh of gratitude to God that yet two hundred more had been delivered from this living hell.

"Then," he continued, "when the planes left, the colonel of our forces called us in, all his sergeant majors, and ordered us out in every direction, to seek out every group of white prisoners. From now on *every* white – not only the men, but women and children too; not only the Americans and Belgians as so far, but every nationality; not only the Catholics, but all religions – *every* white is to be murdered – immediately and mercilessly."

I was sitting there alone in frozen horror.

It was as though he suddenly saw me. Picking up the hurricane lantern from off the table, he swung round on me, holding it close to my face.

"Aren't you the Protestant doctor from Nebobongo?" he asked in surprise.

I could not have answered him, even if I had wanted to do so. "Aren't you Mama Luka?" he queried again, using my African name.

"Yes, she is," answered the leader of the guerrilla group.

"What is she doing here alone?" The sergeant major swung around to face the rebel leader accusingly. "Don't you touch her! She's good. When I was wounded at the beginning of this war, they took me to her hospital, and she healed me!" Saying that, he undid his shirt and showed the two bullet wounds over his breastbone and shoulder.

It was unbelievable, or was it? Was that not just like Almighty God? Fifteen weeks before, He had prepared for this night. He was not taken by surprise, even though I had been. I was not praying to be delivered; I was not thinking in terms of deliverance. I just held on, pleading His Name, knowing that He knew best and would take me through, just asking for grace not to fail Him whatever happened. But He was not dependent on my faith, nor yet on my prayers. Others were praying earnestly; some, as the six missionaries in the next-door house, with understanding and knowledge; others, in lands around the world, with no knowledge of immediate need but under the prompting of the Holy Spirit. That volume of prayer was in accordance with, and so working in co-operation with, His will, as He was preparing to release His power on my behalf.

One minute before that sergeant major was demanding my death. I had not recognized him, but he knew me. Of all the sergeant majors sent out by their colonel in every direction to countless centres of rebel activity, he was the one who came to where we were held, that particular night, at that special hour of that night, to deliver me. Turning to me now, he took me by the hand and led me across the courtyard; he had the guard unlock the door and allow me to join the other six. What a fantastic deliverance – seen from man's limited viewpoint!

Certainly that night prayer turned into praise, and together we thanked God for His gracious intervention on our behalf, marvelling at the wonder of His perfect timing and planning.

Sometimes it may take many years of faithful, persevering prayer before we are allowed to enter into the praise. I remember when I was saying farewells in England before sailing for Congo for the first time in 1953, a lady told me that she had been praying daily for me for thirty years.

"But," I blurted out, startled by her comment, "I'm only twenty-seven years old!"

Thirty years before, she told me, C. T. Studd had written from Congo, asking the home committee to search urgently for a doctor willing to join the small team of missionaries. Since then, she had prayed daily that God would send a missionary doctor to Congo.

"And now I can start praising God that He has answered my prayers," she concluded with a happy smile.

I asked her to keep on praying for me, suspecting a little of the problems that might lie ahead.

When I reached Congo, and began to understand something of the magnitude of the task of setting up a medical service for the WEC area of responsibility, I wrote home to that lady, asking her to redouble her efforts. I shared with her something of the vastness of our territory, the difficulty of travelling on the beaten earth roads during the wet season when they became a sea of mud, the problem of obtaining medicines and equipment from distant cities, the annoyance of things being stolen on the long journey up-country. But above all I underlined the sheer impossibility of *one* person caring for the physical needs of half a million people!

"What we are going to need," I wrote, "is a well-qualified team of national medical auxiliaries. I'm beginning to get excited at the possibility of developing such a team. We could then open up..." and I went on enthusiastically to outline my vision of dispensaries and clinics and care centres all over our region, each run by a medical evangelist, a graduate from this new college. I felt we ought to aim at African leadership of this team just as soon as possible.

"Will you join with me in prayer," I concluded, "that God will guide me and help me in planning the training of such a team: and above all, that He will give us, in the first group of students, the one He has already chosen to be the future leader?"

This week, more than twenty-five years later, I received a prayer letter from the missionary nurse now at Nebobongo, where we opened that first training school. In her letter, she speaks of "John Mangadima, our director" and of "Andrew Asca, the one who does the surgery, in charge of the team in the operating room." John Mangadima was one of the first group of students to train to be a medical evangelist in the WEC school in 1954. Truly today our prayers have turned to praise.

After our rescue by the mercenary forces, and our evacuation to our home countries for rest and rehabilitation, our hearts were torn with distress for those we had left behind. We feared for them, that the rebels would retaliate for our deliverance by even more savage persecution and brutality. Particularly we felt that the lives of our closest friends were at risk, our house helpers and church elders. So we stirred everyone we could at home to pray more earnestly and persistently than ever. For ourselves, we spent many hours in prayer, seeking to be available to the Holy Spirit in His battle against all the forces of evil, *"tying up the strong man"* (Matt. 12:29) and protecting our colleagues and family friends.

At last, news filtered through that the national army, assisted by the mercenary soldiers, had regained control of most of the northeastern province of Zaire, forcing the guerrillas to retreat into small, encircled hideout areas. The way opened for our return. Two of the senior men went first "to spy out the land," and to assure the mission that it was reasonable for women also to go back. Receiving this assurance, two months later three of us women set off by steamer, with a heavily laden Land Rover and trailer, filled with food, clothing and basic necessities for the five of us for at least an initial six-month period. After a long strenuous journey, with seemingly endless problems all along the way, we drove into Nebobongo at 9 a.m. on

Easter Sunday morning and an hour later into Ibambi. Our family were all in church.

Someone heard the throb of the motor.

Could it possibly be them? he thought, slipping out to see. Yes, it was!

The word went back into church: "It's them! It's them!" – and our family poured out in a wild, hilarious sea of joy, hundreds and hundreds of them. It was the most highly moving welcome imaginable. People wept, others laughed. They sang and they cried. They danced for joy, they knelt and praised God for His great goodness. They hugged us until there was hardly anything left to hug! They swept us into the great church, pockmarked from machine-gun firing, yet still standing by God's grace. Together we celebrated Easter with a radiant, resurrection joy of overwhelming happiness. Yes, without doubt, months of believing, persevering prayer had turned into a paean of praise.

But then *we*, who were that day praising God together, had all been rescued. What happened when we paused and thought of those, equally prayed for, who did not come out of the holocaust alive? Had God failed to answer prayer on behalf of Bill and Cyril, the two nurses Winnie and Muriel, the Scots schoolteacher, Jim, and all the many members of other missions? Did God only listen to some prayers? Or were we to believe He said yes to some and no to others, according to capricious whim?

No, God forbid!

God always hears and answers prayer but not necessarily just as we anticipate. As we pray in faith, in the power of His name, seeking to know His will and in obedience to His commands, He answers – according to His perfect will as is best for each one concerned. It is not a matter of *yes* or *no* or even *wait*. As we draw apart into a consciousness of His presence, making ourselves available to the Holy Spirit to pray through us, God is willing to enable us to see things from His viewpoint (even if, as yet, but dimly). We find ourselves burdened to pray for different individuals or situations, as God puts the burden upon our hearts. It rejoices the heart of the Father that we are becoming willing to share the burden that rests on His own heart, and that we desire to be filled with His compassion for the hungry multitude around us. We may not as yet fully comprehend His will in all the fullness of His purposes, but as bit by bit we are enabled to understand something of His burden and to pray accordingly, wanting only His will and to be pleasing to Him, then He graciously answers our prayers beyond all we can ask or think. In this way we can come to know more clearly what God's will really is in a situation, as we watch His answers to our prayers, for these very answers reveal to us His actual will and purpose in that particular situation.

God had a wonderful purpose for Bill and Cyril, Winnie and Muriel, Jim, and many others in taking them home to be with Himself. Their earthly work had been completed. Equally He has a wonderful purpose for each of us who is still here in His service, our earthly work not yet completed.

The prayer for the fulfilment of God's will in the life of each one of us, some saved through suffering for further ministry here on earth, others saved out of the suffering by entrance into His radiant presence in heaven, was answered "Yes!" in each instance, however different the outworking of that answer. By faith we believe this and know it to be true.

"pray exceedingly… wait expectantly"

I have only been able to illustrate the results of prayer by a few chosen incidents where we happen to know the facts involved. On many other occasions, we were keenly conscious of God's intervention on our behalf and "knew" by faith that someone somewhere was praying for us.

The steadier our faith, the more deeply shall we be willing to become involved in "carrying each other's burdens" and the more persistently and perseveringly shall we pray, as we become more and more conscious of what is His perfect will.

Missionary prayer meetings will become more meaningful as we become more deeply interested in the needs of each other. As we read in the newspapers of the murder, let us say, of the president of a little-known country, we shall allow the Spirit to stir us to find out what lies behind the brief announcement. It will take time to look up the geography and present history of the land (in some such book as *Operation World* by Patrick Johnston), and then for the Spirit to reveal to us the specific need of the land as we pray for the appointment of a new president, but it will be time well-spent, with eternal values in view.

When we hear on the radio of, say, a massive exodus of refugees from a land wholly closed to the gospel into a neighbouring country where missionaries and nationals are working to establish local church communities, we shall be stirred to pray earnestly for an outreach to those refugees by local Christians, that many may be reached with the gospel. Thus in turn, they would be enabled to become missionaries to their own people when the time comes for their return home.

As we open our hearts to the facts that surround us – to hear and think and reason with worldwide interest – we give the Holy Spirit the opportunity He seeks to enlighten and burden us with the needs for prayer. As we give ourselves time to be in God's presence, we give the Spirit the opportunity to pray through us for the needs of the world even when we ourselves cannot understand all that is involved.

Missionary prayer meetings could well be likened to the battle for Jericho. As the Israeli men folk marched thirteen times around that walled city in dead silence, they must have been the object of amused ridicule from the amazed inhabitants. The exercise appeared so stupid and totally without rhyme or reason. So may the Islamic world today ridicule the small groups praying for their salvation. Some of the men, in the ancient history of Jericho, doubtless dropped out from the march, footsore and weary, their confidence in Joshua's leadership wavering; but those still marching in obedience on the thirteenth round were there to take possession of the city when the Lord commanded them to shout and the wall collapsed (Josh. 6:1-20)! May we persevere in the practice of prayer, never questioning our captain's leadership, nor being daunted by the world's ridicule, until we see the collapse of the walls of the domains of Satan, and we move in to take the cities for the Lord of Hosts.

By faith the walls of Jericho fell down, after they had been encircled for seven days (Heb. 11:30).

Sometimes our praying will involve faith for relatively "little" things, often things very unimportant in the world's eyes, such as the prayer for the hot water bottle and the dolly, for one individual premature baby and its two-year-old sister in an unknown hospital in the vast interior of Central Africa. We must not despise such "little" things; it is the same faith involved in such praying that works the greatest miracles. This is part of the outworking of Paul's phrase: "pray continually."

How can this be in the midst of our busy lives? Think of the moment when Johnny runs in with thick mud on his boots, just as you finish cleaning the hall carpet. With a gasp of horror at the trail of woe, you are just about to let forth a torrent of frustrated anger on Johnny's unsuspecting head. Well, don't! Think for a second of some busy missionary-housewife, in charge of a large orphanage, with crowds of lads, from toddlers to twelve year-olds. They come tumbling into the home, straight from the football field, bursting with health and fun, to share the latest excitement with a tired and jaded "mother," quite unconscious of the layers of red mud on their bare feet. There is no carpet, but "mother" had just finished scrubbing the concrete floor clean, and her nerves are at the breaking point...

As you pause to pray for her, "Lord, keep her quiet! Help her to keep her temper. Don't let her spoil her testimony by an outburst. In all the heat and weariness, loneliness and frustrations, insecurity and shortages, will You help her to be a real 'mother' to all those boys and girls? May they come to know You through her patient, untiring love..." – suddenly you realize that your own outburst has fizzled out and it is not so bad after all. You can easily rebrush the carpet when the mud dries. And far away, in some forest clearing, on one of the five continents, another mother's heart is quieted, refreshed, and enabled to meet the demands of another hour.

Or perhaps it is late one evening. You have been out at a meeting. As you set off homeward it is dark, cold, and drizzly. You pull your gloves on, turn up your collar and head for the parking lot. You climb into the driver's seat, choke out, ignition on, pull on the starter – and dead silence. You try again ... no response. Aggravated, you get out, open the hood, tap the battery terminals, making sure they are tight and clean. You get back in and try again – still totally unresponsive. Annoyed, you try every known trick, tightening this and cleaning that and adjusting the other. A third try – and an angry realization that you won't win. Locking the door, you set out to walk the twenty minutes home, ready to start muttering against the evil demons that inhabit elderly cars!

Well, don't! Just start thinking (and inevitably then, praying) for that missionary stranded in the jungle, over 100 miles from anywhere. He or she will not be able to call the Automobile Association for help. There is no telephone and no Automobile Association! They dare not wait for aid, as no vehicle may pass that way for several days, and it is the centre of wild elephant country. Something must be done and done successfully at once, if they are to survive.

I got caught in such a situation one night during Christmas 1971. I was driving a two-ton Dodge pickup, heavily laden with print shop machinery. As we ground to a halt, I was fairly certain that our trouble was dirt in the carburettor. Rain was pouring down, and it was very dark and lonely on that stretch of road through the forest. Opening the hood, with a flashlight held in my teeth, I began the routine of taking down and cleaning out the carburettor, the only difference to many similar occasions being that this was my first time in a Dodge vehicle. As I turned the float-chamber upside down to clean it out, I thought I saw something glint by, but it could have been a raindrop caught in the light from the flashlight. I completed the task, returning everything step by step into its due place. Closing the hood, I clambered back into the cab and revved her up. No response. It would not kick over but coughed out into silence every time I took my foot off the accelerator. I went through the whole process again ... with the same results.

You were plodding home through the chilly dark, praying for me.

I suddenly remembered that *something* that had flashed by like a radiant raindrop. I got down in the mud, under the vehicle, and groped for that *something*, not knowing what it was!

You prayed yourself home, hardly noticing the walk in doing so.

I found the lost ball bearing, essential to the working of the slow-running jet in my particular vehicle. I cleaned it, replaced it, revved up and roared away into the night to continue my journey to Ibambi.

It works! You believe in God. You know many missionaries and others in need. You are concerned that God should meet their need. You make yourself available to the Spirit to pray in and through you in accordance with the Father's will, and they are blessed, for He knows their need in detail, though it may be completely unknown to you.

As we become accustomed to "praying continually" for such "little" things, we shall find ourselves more in time to pray for the "big" things such as international and national disasters. As a church we may have prayed during a civil war in some land (such as in Vietnam, in the seventies) but have we continued steadfast in prayer for the suffering church being persecuted in that area even today? As a church we may have prayed at the time of an earthquake disaster (such as in Guatemala or Turkey in recent years) , but are we still praying during the present period of rehabilitation, that the local church may know how to act, as Christ's ambassadors, in the face of continuing suffering, hunger, and poverty? We may have prayed for those responsible for relief programmes in the tragic conditions following some flood disaster (such as in Bangladesh) or coup and counter-coup (such as in Kampuchea). Are we now hardened to news of their continued suffering or disillusioned by the apparent failure of these relief programmes to meet the needs of these suffering people? It is often easy to be stirred up emotionally to start to pray for a situation: but many of us find it very hard to maintain the impetus and to pray effectively and determinedly until the problem is solved.

Probably it is easier for us to pray intelligently when we know some details of the situation needing prayer. In July 1961 when we diagnosed a case of smallpox in our Nebobongo hospital, I was able to get a letter home to my mother immediately telling her our urgent news. She called the community where my sister lived; they bore us up through the following four days and nights, and God stayed the epidemic. We had eight patients in all, the first a little boy, Timothy, and then seven others who had been in close contact with him. It had been a very anxious period of three weeks, while we vaccinated about sixty thousand villagers in the immediate area and waited to see how extensively the disease would spread. I am quite sure that it was the effective, fervent prayers offered on our behalf that caused us to have no further cases.

Since I came home to the United Kingdom from Africa in 1973, I have been travelling extensively, sharing with many, many groups of people the story of God's goodness to us missionaries in Congo (Zaire). During this time I have developed an aggravating degree of motion sickness, be the journey by car or boat or plane. I also began to suffer again from recurrent nightmares, as I had done after our deliverance from the rebellion in 1965, presumably due to reliving in order to recount time after time, in public, some of the harrowing stories of those days in order to share how wonderfully God had kept us and blessed us. I made these two small needs known to a group of friends, asking them to pray daily for me that the travel sickness would not interfere with my ability to fulfil all my engagements, and that God would graciously give me quiet sleep at night, undisturbed by those terrible nightmares. They prayed. God clearly answered. I hardly ever have a nightmare now, and the travel sickness is minimal.

Praying "in the dark," on the other hand, may not always be so easy. However, we do not need to know just how God will work out His plan, nor even exactly what the problem is. We just need to be available to Him, that we may be brought into line with His thoughts so that He may fulfil His perfect will.

On one occasion during my years in Zaire when I was travelling from Nebobongo to Isiro with my African friend Susan Kaniki, we were following a huge twelve-ton cotton truck towing a ten-ton trailer, both packed to capacity. Rounding a corner near the foot of Deti hill we began the long steep climb, the sandy crest of the road falling away into deep gullies on either side. Part way up the hill, closely behind the cotton transport, I was suddenly seized with an urgent feeling that I should return to the foot of the hill. I halted the van, put it into reverse, and eased my way backwards, rounding the corner and pulling off to the side of the road in a small clearing. Susan looked at me, puzzled, when suddenly we heard a tremendous crash ahead. We leaped out of the van, and ran forward, round the corner, to see the trailer jack-knifed across the road, over on its side. It was obvious that it had become detached from the main vehicle, had careered down the hill backwards, out of all control, and had caught a wheel in the ditch, bringing it to its crashing halt. If we had not reversed down that hill when we did, we would probably both have been killed. Silent and awed, we returned to our car and thanked God for His great goodness to us – and I wondered who had been praying at that moment. They could not have known what our need was, and yet urged by the Spirit, they must have prayed for us that God would keep us and protect us in His perfect will.

Obviously I can frustrate this pattern of divine intervention, but this does not alter the fact of God's desire to answer earnest, believing prayer. On another occasion, again with Susan as my companion, the outcome was very different. We had travelled through a day and night the 350 miles to Kisangani, the capital city of our province. Two rather fruitless days had been spent in the city trying to buy goods that were not available and trying to meet expected visitors from a plane on which they had not travelled! On Friday afternoon, we set out to return home, travelling through the night against the earnest advice of others who knew how grossly tired I was. These friends (and maybe others) prayed for us. At 5 a.m., we had a terrible crash. I had fallen asleep at the wheel and left the road at thirty miles an hour. The vehicle was a total wreck, and Susan and I narrowly escaped death.

The prayers of my friends did not prevent that accident – but we were alive. Shocked at how nearly I had caused Susan's death as well as my own, I trust that as a result of that terrifying experience I was humble enough to listen more readily to the advice of others thereafter.

✧ ✦ ✧ ✦ ✧ ✦ ✧

May each one of us be more and more ready to be stirred by the Holy Spirit to pray – to pray continually –

To learn to pray exceedingly

with "requests, prayers, intercession, and thanksgiving ... for everyone" everywhere, under all conditions and in every type of need.

And this is the confidence which we have: that, before Him, if we ask anything according to His will, He hears us (1 John 5:14).

How do we know if we are praying 'according to His will'? He sees the motives of our hearts. If I sincerely want His will, even though my prayer may be wrongly worded or my expectation of His answer may be wrongly directed, He *will* answer "according to His will." Thus by watching the answers to my prayers, I can learn to understand more clearly and accurately what is His will. Thus gradually my praying will become more in line with His will, as He enables me to think His thoughts and see His plan. Granted that my heart motive in prayer is honestly "not my will but Yours be done," when an answer to prayer is not what I expected it to be, that will show me, that in that instance, I had not properly understood His will. His answers to sincere praying reveal to us His will.

To learn to wait expectantly

will become the attitude of my heart in the practice of prayer, that I may thereby discover His perfect will in each situation.

> Stir me, oh! stir me, Lord, Thy heart was stirred
> By love's intensest fire, till Thou didst give
> Thine only Son, Thy best beloved One,
> E'en to the dreadful cross, that I might live.
> Stir me to give myself so back to Thee,
> That Thou canst give Thyself again through me.

EPILOGUE

FAITH – OUR GIVING TO GOD

And what more shall I say? I do not have time to tell about Gideon, Barak, Samson, Jephthah, David, Samuel and the prophets, who through faith conquered kingdoms, administered justice, and gained what was promised; who shut the mouths of lions, quenched the fury of the flames, and escaped the edge of the sword; whose weakness was turned to strength; and who became powerful in battle and routed foreign armies. Women received back their dead, raised to life again. Others were tortured and refused to be released, so that they might gain a better resurrection. Some faced jeers and flogging, while still others were chained and put in prison. They were stoned; they were sawn in two; they were put to death by the sword. They went about in sheepskins and goatskins, destitute, persecuted and mistreated – the world was not worthy of them. They wandered in deserts and mountains, and in caves and holes in the ground.

These were all commended for their faith, yet none of them received what had been promised. God had planned something better for us, so that only together with us would they be made perfect (Heb. 11:32-40 NIV).

At the beginning of this book we tried to answer the question: "What *is* faith?" and we saw faith as God's gift to us by which He establishes a living relationship between Himself and us. Faith is a fact, though it has to be appreciated by us, at least to some extent, by our emotional reactions. Faith can be thought of as a sixth sense, by which we can relate to the unseen world of the spirit, in much the same way as our five physical senses relate us to the seen world around us.

This faith sense can grow in us, until our appreciation of the things of God is as acute and real as our physical appreciation of the natural things of the seen world, in much the same way as a child's sense of hearing develops until he can speak plainly.

Nevertheless the fact of faith does not grow. Faith is. God gives us faith as a gift when we are born again into His family, and thereby we "know" Him.

The fact that the world is round was unaltered by centuries of man's unbelief, but once the fact was acknowledged, man began to develop further understanding, such as the use of the sextant in navigation. Similarly, we need to ask God to "stir up" our faith, that we may develop our understanding of His will and purpose.

Then we looked briefly at some of the fruits of faith. As our faith relationship with God expands, we find ourselves growing from childhood to adulthood as Christians. The initial joy of receiving gifts from God to supply needs in our lives – physical, mental, material and spiritual – change to a joy in giving an allegiance to God of loving loyalty in all circumstances. As faith grows in us, we find it our greatest joy to serve Him, and we find ourselves no longer dependent on Gods "giving" visible gifts to us, but rather wholly dependent on His gift of Himself to us,

A second fruit of faith is the ability to hear God's voice directing us in our daily lives. By faith we become sensitive to His promptings through reading and studying the Bible, through the advice of older Christian friends, through the combination of circumstances, guiding us into the path that He has planned for us. Faith enables us to believe that God has prepared a path for each of us, and that He desires to lead us into and along that pathway.

A third fruit of faith is the desire to pray. We find ourselves wanting to talk with God. This is sheer folly to the man without faith. It is part of the outcome of faith in the Christian's heart. We begin to want to tell God that we love Him and to bring our needs to Him. There is so much that puzzles us in learning to live as God would have us live, that we must ask for His help. Just as a child is full of questions, bombarding mother and father with an endless stream of "Why ...?" and "How ...?" in order to grow and develop in the natural world, so God has given us the privilege of prayer that we may come to Him with all our requests that we may grow in the spiritual realm. Above all, it is by praying and watching the answers to our prayers, that we learn to understand God's will, and we begin to think with His thoughts and see things from His viewpoint. By prayer He can mould us to the image of His Son, as He wants to do.

And what more can I say?

God's gift of faith in my heart, manifesting itself by many fruits such as a spirit of giving, dependence on Him for guidance and a desire to pray, must stir in me a great longing to respond in some way. I want to give God something in return, as a way of saying thank you.

Yet what have I to give?

The hymn writer caught this sense of yearning:

Stir me to give *myself* so back to Thee
That Thou can'st give Thyself again through me.

The first part of the verse reminds us again of the great love that stirred God's heart on our behalf:

> ... till Thou didst give
> Thine only Son, Thy best beloved One,
> E'en to the dreadful cross, that I might live,

or we might paraphrase that ending: "that I might have faith to know that I live in the spiritual realm." It is this *living faith* that prompts the yearning of the last two lines.

This is what prompted "Gideon, Barak, Samson, Jephthah, David, Samuel, and the prophets" to the exploits listed for us in glorious profusion in the eleventh chapter of the letter to the Hebrews. Faith is that gift of God, put into the heart of each one who truly believes in Him, that enables us to laugh at impossibilities and then to watch God conquer the invincible.

In the Old Testament Abraham's wife, Sarah, when she was "old, advanced in age ... Sarah was past childbearing," yet gave birth to Isaac. A glorious contrast between human inability and divine power! When the promise of divine intervention was first made, Sarah laughed in human unbelief, which was the result of logical reasoning and limitations of experience. She may have wondered if God were perhaps ignorant of the facts, but at least she knew that *this* promise could not be fulfilled. Then God reiterated the promise, making it quite clear that He knew what He was talking about, and Sarah realized that it was not a mistake. Her doubts slowly changed to faith, and she found herself expecting Him to fulfil His promise. When the divine power was experienced, in answer to that rising tide of faith, Sarah laughed again, but now in wondering awe. Indeed she called her son Isaac, which means "laughter," saying: "God has made laughter for me; everyone who hears will laugh with me." Truly, as the writer to the Hebrews tells us, this was the laugh of faith:

> *By faith even Sarah herself received ability to conceive even beyond the proper time of life, since she considered Him faithful who had promised* (Gen. 18:9-15; 21:1-7; Heb. 11: 11).

In the New Testament, Paul expresses the same attitude of triumphant faith in the eighth chapter of his letter to the Romans, verses 28-39. Having reminded us of the impossibility of being separated from the love of Christ even by trouble or hardship or persecution, famine or nakedness, danger or sword, or yet by false accusations or condemnations, he declares that, even if facing death all day long, he cannot doubt God's word that:

> *…in all these things we overwhelmingly conquer through Him who loved us.*

What a shout of triumph! Faith gives us the assurance of triumph in the face of every difficulty and all that would speak of defeat.

> *Faith is the assurance of things hoped for, the conviction of things not seen* (Heb. 11:1).

It is a way of life that is pleasing to God.

> *Without faith it is impossible to please Him, for he who comes to God must believe that He is and that He is a rewarder of those who seek Him* (Heb. 11:6).

Faith is a way of life that must be followed with confident perseverance until we enter into the full possession of the reward.

> *Therefore, since we have so great a cloud of witnesses, let us also lay aside every encumbrance and the sin which so easily*

entangles us, and let us run with endurance the race that is set before us (Heb. 12:1).

Faith is exciting to a Christian. It is a blank cheque duly signed by God, giving the drawer access to the unlimited riches of heavenly grace. We can take "by faith" all that God has prepared for us in His abundant, outpoured generosity, as we endorse the "check" by prayer and faith, presenting it to our heavenly Father in accordance with His will.

"Things which eye has not seen and ear has not heard, and – which have not entered the heart of Man. All that God has prepared for those who love Him. For to us God revealed them through the Spirit" (1 Cor. 2:9-10).

To the worldly-wise person, following human reasoning and banking on his meagre experience through his five senses, all this may seem utterly foolish or even presumptuous. It is impossible without faith to understand the ways of faith. The man of faith must not be surprised or depressed that he cannot help the worldly man to comprehend these ways of God. It is just not possible. God Himself has told us this:

Where is the wise man? Where is the scribe? Where is the debater of this age? Has not God made foolish the wisdom of the world? For since in the wisdom of God, the world through its wisdom did not come to know God, God was well-pleased through the foolishness of the message preached to save those who believe. For indeed Jews ask for signs, and Greeks search for wisdom, but we preach Christ crucified, to Jews a stumbling block, and to Gentiles foolishness, but to those who are the called, both Jews and Greeks, Christ the power of God and the wisdom of God. Because the foolishness of God is wiser than men, and the weakness of God is stronger than men (1 Cor. 1:20-25).

We have referred earlier to Moses' faith in God, when he left Pharaoh's household and became identified with the despised Israelites because *"he regarded disgrace for the sake of Christ as of greater value than the treasures of Egypt, because he was looking ahead to his reward"* (Heb. 11:26). By faith, throughout the period of the plagues, Moses stood up to Pharaoh ten times. By faith he led the people of Israel out of Egypt to the shores of the Red Sea. Sandwiched between the sea on the one hand and the advancing Egyptian host on the other, by faith, in obedience to God's command, Moses raised his rod toward the sea. The waters divided, leaving a pathway of dry ground from one shore to the other, and he led the two and a half million people over to safety. The Egyptian army, attempting to follow them, drowned as the waters returned to their normal course.

Shortly after this miraculous deliverance, the whole Israelite community were moving slowly through the desert, skirting the Sinai peninsula, when they arrived at Rephidim. They began to set up camp for a night's rest, *"and there was no water for the people to drink"* (Exod. 17:1).

They quarrelled with Moses, demanding water to drink!

He, in annoyance, told them that their quarrel was not with him, but with God.

The people in their thirst became unreasonable and tempers began to rise, until they threatened to stone Moses, making him the scapegoat of their impotent frustration.

Moses cried out to God in alarm and fear, but also in instinctive faith that God could and would take over. That is how faith often works, being sparked into activity by a contrary or frightening situation. In no way did the fear, Moses' first reaction to the anger of the people, reveal a failure of faith. That fear was a normal, reasonable, human reaction. His immediate recourse to God crying out for help, demonstrated the reality of his faith, rather than the lack of it! His fear triggered off faith, rather than panic.

"Pass before the people," the LORD *commanded Moses, in response to his cry. "Take in your hand your staff with which you struck the Nile, and go. Behold, I will stand before you there on the rock at Horeb ....Strike the rock and water will come out of it, that the people may drink."*

The Bible simply states: *"And Moses did so"* (Exod. 17:1-7).

What a fantastic story! What unbelievable, naked faith!

Supposing that it had not worked? What a fool Moses would have looked in the eyes of all the people ... But God is faithful and never fails. God stood by Moses in Egypt and at the Red Sea. He would not let him down now.

Moses first cried out in fear, then he listened, believed God, and *obeyed.*

God heard and spoke and acted – honouring Moses' faith and obedience.

✧✦✧✦✧✦✧

"Stir me, oh! stir me Lord ... to give myself ... back to Thee"

When Moses came down from his forty days in the presence of God on Mount Sinai filled with the vision of the Tabernacle, the tent of meeting, where God would meet with and commune with His people, he called on all the Israelites to become involved in the great task of construction. All were to *give* all they could. Moses had seen God at work in all that had occurred in his nation's history, and now he saw a chance to *give* something to God to express their gratitude.

"This is what the Lord has commanded: Take from what you have, an offering for the Lord.. Everyone who is willing to bring to the Lord...," and then he listed the treasures only the rich would own – gold, silver, and bronze; blue, purple, and scarlet yarn and fine linen. The poor – the majority – might have shrugged their shoulders, feeling that this was no concern of theirs; unfortunately that is the attitude of many churchgoing people today when they hear a challenge to personal involvement in evangelism at home or overseas!

But Moses took them by surprise when he told them of the next object that would be needed in the construction of the Tabernacle: "goat hair." Anyone could bring that! They did not even have to own the goat. The hair was caught on the thorns of every bush in that desert area, and merely needed to be collected. Not only the tall, but the short could give this offering; not only the clever, but the dull could collect and bring it in.

"All who are skilled among you are to come and make everything the Lord has commanded." Moses continued, listing all the furniture as well as the basic structure of the Tabernacle and its courtyard, even down to the hundreds of tent pegs that would be needed.

> *"And,"* we read, *"all the congregation of the children of Israel departed from the presence of Moses. And they came, everyone whose heart stirred him up, and every one whom his spirit made willing, and they brought the* LORD's *offering to the work ..."* (Exod. 35:20-21 KJV).

"All" had to be involved, everyone whose heart stirred him up was to come and give what he could to the service of the Lord.

So today the Holy Spirit would continue to stir us up to give ourselves, all we have and are, to the work of the building of the Temple of God, that temple not made with hands, but made of living stones, men and women throughout the world whose hearts have been turned to Him in living faith. We are exhorted to give ourselves, sharing our very lives with those who have not yet heard or responded to the gospel.

"Having thus a fond affection for you," Paul said, when writing to the young church at Thessalonica, *"we were well-pleased to impart to you not only the gospel of God but also our own lives, because you had become very dear to us"* (1 Thess. 2:8).

All Christians, not just a select few, are made new creatures in Christ Jesus and thereafter called to become His ambassadors, entrusted with the word of reconciliation – sent out to represent our Lord and to teach His message throughout the world. Christ's last command to us, before He ascended back into heaven, was that we should be His witnesses *"in Jerusalem, and in all Judea and Samaria, and even to the remotest part of the earth"* (Acts 1:8).

God gives His gift of *faith* to *be* Christian witnesses, His ambassadors – not just to give, to go, to pray, but to be. We are to be available to God all the time, so that we can act in obedience (giving what He commands us); so that we can challenge the powers of darkness (going where He sends us); and so that we can keep on believing in the midst of every type of discouragement (praying as He burdens us). In all of this, our faith will be tried, as gold by fire – purifying, refining, enriching it – as we translate faith into service for Him.

"Blessed be the God and Father of our Lord Jesus Christ" says Peter in his first letter. *"According to His great mercy He has*

caused us to be born again" through faith. Then he continues, referring to this faith: *"...in this you greatly rejoice, even though now for a little while, if necessary, you have been distressed by various trials that the proof of your faith, being more precious than gold, which is perishable, may be found to result in praise and glory and honour at the revelation of Jesus Christ."*

By faith we give ourselves wholly back to God to be available for the outworking of His perfect will. It is the presence of faith in our hearts that makes us want to give ourselves back to Him. I remember learning about this aspect of faith when I was a candidate at our mission's headquarters, but it has taken many years of service to begin to appreciate the full import of that teaching. Our director spoke of faith as the next most important faculty to love. To quote his words: "Where love motivates, faith acts. Faith carries out the urges of love."

We were taught that faith is the capacity to receive that which God gives and to use and apply it. We know that God does give and provide all that we need, but His gifts would be meaningless if we did not accept them, and put them to use. We should be like the proverbial horse that can be led to the water but cannot be forced to drink. God provides us with food necessary for our health, but we must take it and eat it, if it is to benefit us. We are surrounded by fresh air, but we must breathe.

As by faith, we appropriate God's gift of pardoning grace and of power to be His witnesses, so we can make our response, in obedience to His command to *"go and tell all nations."* As we become involved with the Lord in this ministry of *"feeding the multitudes,"* we shall begin to understand something of the burden on God's heart for the needs of a lost world and to pray that He will fill our hearts with His compassion for them.

"When He ... saw a great multitude, He felt compassion for them, because they were like sheep without a shepherd" – so Mark recalls the incident in his gospel. And although Christ was tired and needed rest, nevertheless *"He began to teach them many things"* (Mark 6:34).

Today our Saviour looks out on a vaster crowd than ever – three thousand million people without the knowledge of His love. As then, so now, His heart is moved with compassion and He looks for those whom He can send to them as His ambassadors.

The disciples reminded the Lord on that occasion that evening was drawing near, and the folk needed to be sent on their way if they were to get home before dark or to buy food before the stores closed.

"But," the Lord responded to His disciples, *"you give them something to eat."*

Not unnaturally they were shattered at the illogicality of the suggestion! They had nothing there, no food, no kitchen ... no committee or sub-committee that we would consider essential to get anything achieved. It was a remote place. Had not the Lord Himself deliberately chosen such a place so that they could be alone?

"That would take eight months of a man's wages!" they replied incredulously. *"Are we to go and spend that much on bread and give it to them to eat?"*

"How many loaves do you have?" He asked. *"Go and see."* We look at our resources today in the same way and find them pitifully inadequate. How can we go against the massive might of militant Islam in our puny strength? Or against the impressive intellectual powers of the modern atheistic world in our poor wisdom?

When the disciples had investigated their meagre resources, they told the Lord, *"Five – and two fish,"* and they gave them into the Master's hands, just a lad's lunch of rolls and sardines. Pitiful!

What faith it takes to believe that it is worth giving God our infinitesimally small resources when faced with the needs of the world! How hard it is to stir up the faith of the church everywhere to give Him all we have and to see what He can do with it. Our giving is still in such an embryo stage, an odd gift here and there as it occurs to us, or even perhaps a regular tithing of all our earnings; but as yet we know practically nothing of the sort of giving that Jesus commended. When the poor widow put two very small copper coins into the Temple treasury, Jesus said that she had put in more than all the others, even than the rich who "were putting in large sums." How then did Jesus measure what was given? By what was left!

"They all put in out of their surplus," He said, "but she, out of her poverty, put in all she owned, all she had to live on" (Mark 12:41-44).

Our Lord longs for us to have faith to give Him all we are and have, presenting ourselves as living sacrifices to Him that He may do with us what He will, as the lad apparently gave his whole lunch. We do not read that he kept back half for himself, fearful that he get no return for his giving. We do not read that he gave only ninety-five per cent of his lunch. The Bible knows nothing of that type of giving. God asks of us *all*. He want us to love Him with all our hearts and minds and souls and strength. He wants us, as Peter, to forsake *all* to follow the Master who will then make us fishers of men. He wants us, as Paul, to count *all* else as worth less than refuse, that we may win Christ and be found in Him. May that "all" bite deeply into our hearts, stirring our faith to trust our all to Him.

Jesus took the loaves and fish from the hands of His disciples. He made the people sit down in orderly groups. Then *"He took the five loaves and the two fish, and looking up toward heaven, He blessed the food and broke the loaves and He kept giving them to the disciples to set before them; and He divided up the two fish among them all."*

Jesus did not Himself take the bread and the fish to the crowds. No. He blessed them, broke them and gave them back to His disciples, who then were sent to distribute them. Think of the faith that needed! And we need faith to believe when He hands back to us those beggarly resources that we bring to Him, and asks us to take them out to the multitudes. Our Lord did not even give the disciples a *whole* loaf each; no. He gave each one a broken loaf. That first step, with their backs to the Master and facing the sceptical crowd, with just half a broken loaf in their hands, must have demanded tremendous faith – faith that the Lord Himself gave to them!

There is the secret!

Can we trust the Lord to stir up in us that kind of faith today, so that we will obey Him and at His command will go wherever He sends us? The crowd in front of us today is no less sceptical, often downright cynical and ready to pour ridicule, if not abuse, upon us. The crowd before us may be angry and militant, powerful followers of another creed; or it may be wholly indifferent and apathetic. It may be subtle, concealing hidden darts of hatred with flattery; it may be bitter with jealousy, determined to nullify by any means at all any approach made to it. This crowd may be near at home – our own kith and kin; or it may be thousands of miles away across cultural barriers of practice and language. Dare we go? Dare we encourage today's Christian young people in all our churches worldwide to go wherever the Lord sends with a like spirit of whole-hearted obedience?

Jesus said, "As the Father has sent me, I also send you" (John 20:21).

Why was Christ sent to the world by the Father?
That He might seek and save the lost; that He might give His life a ransom for many. And this is why today He would send us to the world, that through us He might continue to seek and to save the lost as we give our lives to Him in their service.

Where was Christ sent by the Father?
To the world of sinners. And so He would send us to the world of sinful men and women in the uttermost parts of the earth or on our own doorsteps, men and women in all their sophistication or degradation, in their pathetic wealth or abject poverty, in the midst of their economic and industrial progress or in their primitive underdevelopment. He sends us to every place where man dwells, to represent Him, to tell of His love and pardon for those who truly repent of their sins – sent as His ambassadors with the word of reconciliation. If we believe that they are perishing, three thousand million of them, dying without Christ, shall we not be constrained by love to go and tell them of the Saviour, the only One who can redeem the lost?

How was Christ sent by the Father?
He went voluntarily as a servant – humble, obedient, submissive to His Father's will. That is how He would send each one of us out into the world today to serve mankind, asking for no reward save that of knowing that we do His will. We shall give Christ the unconditional surrender of

our wills and rights and unquestioning obedience to the least prompting of His Spirit, and we shall know an ever-growing sense of privilege filling our hearts that we have been called of God to such service.

We need faith to believe that in His grace He has chosen to use such as we are, as distributing channels of His abundant, loving supply to meet the overwhelming needs of the world. We need faith too that we may encourage other Christians everywhere to become burdened and involved also, longing and praying earnestly with a deep sense of responsibility for the fulfilment of God's purposes for the world for which He died.

> *Paul said, "I have been crucified with Christ, and it is no longer I who live, but Christ lives in me, and the life which I now live in the flesh I live by faith in the Son of God, who loved me, and delivered Himself up for me"* (Gal. 2:20).

Day by day we must bring to the Lord the empty vessels of our lives that He may indwell and fill them, that there may be an ever-increasing overflow of blessing upon those around us.

> Stir me to give myself so back to Thee
> That Thou canst give Thyself again through me.

And as this happens, the triumphant words of the last verse of this searching hymn will be our constant prayer also:

> Stir me, oh! stir me, Lord, for I can see
> Thy glorious triumph-day begin to break;
> The dawn already gilds the eastern sky:
> Oh, Church of Christ, arise, awake, awake;
> Oh, stir us, Lord, as heralds of that day,
> For night is past, our King is on His way.

About the Author

Dr. Helen Roseveare was born in Hailebury, Herts, England in 1925. Although she was deeply religious, she had neither the understanding nor the assurance of salvation. She was converted during her medical studies at Cambridge University through the ministry of the Christian Union, an association of evangelical university students.

In 1951, she joined WEC International and served in the Belgian Congo (now Democratic Republic of Congo) as a medical missionary. She was used of God in previously existing ministries, as well as to begin new works for the extension of the medical and spiritual ministries to the people of Democratic Republic of Congo.

During the Simba rebellion of the 1960s, Dr. Roseveare was one of many missionaries captured and mistreated by the rebel soldiers. God used these harsh experiences, coupled with other lessons learned before and after the rebellion, to give her the ministry she has today.

Dr. Roseveare is retired from WEC International and lives in Northern Ireland.

WEC (Worldwide Evangelization for Christ) is an international, interdenominational mission agency committed to planting the Church of Jesus Christ among the least evangelized people groups. At the time of this printing, WEC numbers approximately 2000 missionaries from 45 nationalities serving in over 70 countries.

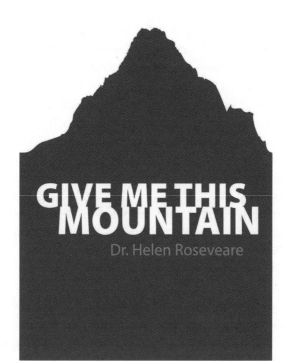

GIVE ME THIS MOUNTAIN

Dr. Helen Roseveare

Give Me This Mountain
Helen Roseveare

A well-known missionary doctor and author, with several of her works still in print, she worked in the north-eastern province of the Belgian Congo with the Heart of Africa Mission in the 1950's & 60's. She established a substantial pioneer medical service and assisted the churches before Congo's independence in 1960, and continued there for some years after, at a time when many had to flee for their lives.

Helen tells her story in down to earth terms, from playing cricket for the ladies' university side (a liberated woman even then), to her return to Britain after five months as a hostage in rebel terrorist hands. Her candid account is an antidote to any delusion that missionaries are saints who float about an inch off the ground, and see a blinding light from heaven when they receive 'the call'. She almost failed in missionary school through her personal failings. Her own admitted stubbornness, pride, know-it-all attitude, and inability to work with others made her a liability. The final decision to send her overseas came when an incident with a broken washing line proved that she at least had a sense of humour in the face of adversity!

Physical dangers and her personal ambition in the Congo often almost sank her, but her faith and hard work brought her through. Her story is one of bright mountains, conquered after experiencing the dark valleys and learning to give the glory to God.

ISBN 978-1-84550-189-1

HE GAVE US A VALLEY

Dr. Helen Roseveare

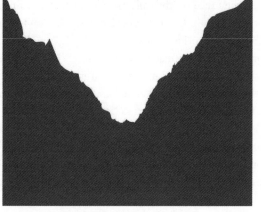

He Gave Us a Valley
Helen Roseveare

After twelve years of missionary work in the northeast province of what was the Belgian Congo, building up a simple medical service, civil war erupted with horrific effects. During the war Helen was brutally beaten and raped and left with no choice but to return to Britain (this story is told in '*Give me this Mountain*').

She quickly returned to the Congo in 1966 to assist in the rebuilding of the nation. She helped establish a new medical school and hospital (for the other hospitals that she built were destroyed) and served there until 1973. In the eight years following the war, despite endless frustrations, again and again God showed his unfailing guidance and unstinted provision for her needs. This book is the story of the joys and adventures of re-establishing the medical work, the church building programme and the work of forgiveness, necessary after the destruction of the civil war.

ISBN 978-1-84550-190-7

DIGGING
DITCHES
THE LATEST CHAPTER OF
AN INSPIRATIONAL LIFE

HELEN ROSEVEARE

Digging Ditches
The Latest Chapter of an Inspirational Life
Helen Roseveare

Helen Roseveare, affectionately called Mama Luka, pioneered vital medical work in the Rain forests of the Belgian Congo - now the Democratic Republic of Congo.

Throughout her eight years in training for the mission field and her first twelve years in Congo Helen Roseveare had prayed that God would give her a mountain top experience of his glory and power. However, after enduring civil war and having to start from the beginning again, and later when caring for her elderly mother, she realised that God's work is done in the valleys.

He gives us the valleys and we are to dig the ditches (2 Kings 3:16), trusting that they will be filled with life-giving water at the appropriate time.

This is an inspiring story because it shows those times when God's blessings seem withdrawn - they are subsequently shown to have been there **all the time.**

If you have ever experienced times when God's call on your life seems remote, or you are encountering trials and problems, you will find refreshment from Helen's pen. She shows how 'trusting in the Lord' can be a gritty, rewarding drama rather than a wispy platitude.

ISBN 978-1-84550-058-0

DR. HELEN ROSEVEARE

*"Each time I read one of her accounts, I want
to be like her, I want to know God as she does."*
Noël Piper

LIVING
SACRIFICE

WILLING TO BE
WHITTLED AS
AN ARROW

Living Sacrifice
Willing to be Whittled as an Arrow
Helen Roseveare

Sacrifice is a term of the past, not of today. Today, no one is expected to sacrifice anything. We are surrounded by game shows that give you riches if you answer a few questions on general knowledge or guess the right box to open. The unspoken spirit of the age is 'if something is difficult, do something else instead. If something is expensive, borrow it or borrow the money to buy it'.

What place does 'sacrifice' have in this world?

The Bible says it is central - and that sacrifice is not only a vital key to the future, it is the essence of a Christian's life, today.

The books in Dr. Helen Roseveare's 'Living...' series have become instant classics. If you pick up this book anywhere and start to read it, you won't be able to put it down as she skilfully weaves stories of sacrifice together with Christian teaching on the subject.

If those words sound alien to you then you may not have yet entered into the joy of Christian belief and service. The key to an authentic life is sacrifice.

Helen Roseveare has led an incident-filled life as a medical missionary. A best-selling author, she is still active in writing and in demand for international conferences on mission and faith.

ISBN 978-1-84550-294-2

• Helen Roseveare •

ON HIS MAJESTY'S SERVICE

Irene Howat

Helen Roseveare: On His Majesty's Service
Trailblazers Series
Irene Howat

Helen Roseveare qualified as a doctor, packed up her life in England and set off to be a missionary in the belgian congo (now the Democratic Republic of Congo). She went there to set up hospitals and rural clinics and train national nurses to work in them. Her work often took Helen on long journeys through dense forests on roads that would make a fairground ride seem tame!

After Congo became an independent country Helen's service was interrupted by the Simba Rebellion, during which she was assaulted and held captive for several months.

After some time of recovery Helen went back to the renamed 'Zaire' to serve the Lord by working with people there. In the years that followed she established a nurses' training college in the hope that the nurses', midwives and health workers who trained there would spread out through the vast northeast region of the country, taking the good news of the Lord Jesus Christ with them.

Since returning to the UK, Helen has become well known as a conference speaker. Her experiences in Africa have been an encouragement to many and made her well known and loved throughout the world.

Irene Howat is an award-winning author who is accomplished writer in writing for children and adults. She has many titles to her name. She is married to a minister and they have a grown up family. She is also a talented artist and lives in Argyll, Scotland. She especially enjoys letters from children and replies to all of them!

ISBN 978-1-84550-259-1

Christian Focus Publications

Our mission statement –

STAYING FAITHFUL

In dependence upon God we seek to impact the world through literature faithful to His infallible Word, the Bible. Our aim is to ensure that the Lord Jesus Christ is presented as the only hope to obtain forgiveness of sin, live a useful life and look forward to heaven with Him.

Our books are published in four imprints:

CHRISTIAN
FOCUS

Popular works including biographies, commentaries, basic doctrine and Christian living.

CHRISTIAN
HERITAGE

Books representing some of the best material from the rich heritage of the church.

MENTOR

Books written at a level suitable for Bible College and seminary students, pastors, and other serious readers. The imprint includes commentaries, doctrinal studies, examination of current issues and church history.

CF4•K

Children's books for quality Bible teaching and for all age groups: Sunday school curriculum, puzzle and activity books; personal and family devotional titles, biographies and inspirational stories – because you are never too young to know Jesus!

Christian Focus Publications Ltd,
Geanies House, Fearn, Ross-shire,
IV20 1TW, Scotland, United Kingdom.
www.christianfocus.com